Virgo

The Ultimate Guide to an Amazing Zodiac Sign in Astrology

Your Free Gift (only available for a limited time)

Thanks for getting this book! If you want to learn more about various spirituality topics, then join Mari Silva's community and get a free guided meditation MP3 for awakening your third eye. This guided meditation mp3 is designed to open and strengthen ones third eye so you can experience a higher state of consciousness. Simply visit the link below the image to get started.

https://spiritualityspot.com/meditation

Contents

Introduction

An understanding of astrology can alter your life. It has done so for many other people across the planet; me included. Astrology brings the hidden corners of your entire being to light. It is a way to expand your awareness of yourself and others. Your compassion for yourself and your environment depends on it. Your past grows much clearer, and you get a glimpse of your possible future.

Astrology can alter your perception. Once you understand your place in the stars, it becomes impossible to perceive the world like you used to. This field is filled with terms just as poetic as they are objective, fueling your curiosity, and stimulating your intellect. As you probe deeper into the mystical ways of astrology, every human is transformed into a mystery waiting to be understood.

The crown of it all is that astrology presents an unmatched way of discovering yourself not just as a member of a zodiac sign, but as a personalized assortment of abilities and qualities. You are someone whose personal essence reflects the cosmos. Many individuals believe that astrology merely categorizes people into twelve places, but they couldn't be more wrong! Astrology teaches that every one of us is liable to be subjected to universal desires and needs, and that we are all completely and exquisitely unique.

Astrology is as old as time itself and is a constantly evolving system that possesses a variety of dimensions and can be perceived in several forms, from Chinese astrology to Vedic astrology or Western astrology. This book is centered on the Virgo zodiac sign of Western astrology, but it also has many sublevels, branching off into other zodiac signs when the need arises.

Astrology is an unbiased tool used to understand others and yourself. It is used to embrace opportunities, confront adversity, analyze relationships, and make simple choices. For centuries, man has been very fascinated with the stars and the way they affect us all. It's only natural for you to be intrigued by astrology; to wonder about all the many ways these heavenly bodies might affect your day-to-day life.

If you're reading this book, then it means you're particularly captivated by the Virgo — if you aren't one yourself. Whether you're a Virgo, or you're simply seeking to understand the Virgo in your life, you are in luck! This book contains all you need to know about the zodiac's Virgo sign.

Finally, astrology has nothing to do with predestination or fate. It leans more toward propensity and possibility. It is more about maximizing your strong points and acknowledging your weak ones. With astrology, you can finally understand people and align yourself with the universe. Like Sir Francis Bacon once said, "The stars do not compel, they impel." No truer words have been said.!

Chapter One: An Introduction to the Virgo

When you say to people, "I'm a Virgo," you're usually talking about your Sun sign. What's a Sun sign, you ask? When the Sun goes around the Earth year after year, it passes through the zodiac's twelve signs, taking a month in each one.

As for astrology, the Sun is a planet. You could call it the most powerful planet, and you'd be right. In terms of horoscopes, the Sun has the most influence in how others perceive you, how you express yourself, and the motivations and reasons you have for wanting to achieve the goals you've set for yourself.

Your Sun sign offers a big-picture depiction of your personality. Think of it as the outline of a drawing before it's filled in with more details. To have a general idea of yourself as a Virgo, or of your Virgo friend or family member, then the Sun sign will give you what you need to know.

If you've ever read up on Virgo astrology and felt, "Well, that doesn't seem particularly accurate," it's because your Sun sign only gives you the foundation of your personality. Other than the Sun, there's the Moon to consider. A study of your birth chart would likely show that the Moon is in a much different zodiac sign altogether than the Sun.

All planets within your birth chart can be of a different sign, and this makes you a complex, unique individual. Imagine if all Virgos were the same! That would make for a not so fun world — not that Virgos aren't fun. They're amazing - once they let you in.

The only path to know who you are is to look closely at the whole birth chart rather than just focus on your Sun sign. Even when you have all the information you need, understand that you're human. This means you're a dynamic being.

The signs may show you the type of person you are, but in the end, you get to say what you are and what you become. However, knowing the attributes of a Virgo will go far in helping you have better relationships with them. If you're a Virgo yourself, it will help you understand yourself and how you can connect with the world around you in a mutually beneficial way.

Sun Signs and Their Divisions

Before we dive into the Virgo fully, I must help you understand the zodiac signs' various groupings and divisions. We begin with dualities.

Dualities

All twelve zodiacs belong to either the masculine or the feminine, with six falling under each category. We know this grouping as duality. While there are certain preconceptions about what it means to be masculine or feminine, this doesn't imply that one is better than the other. Think of them as neutral qualities, and little more.

The feminine is magnetic and receptive and has nothing to do with being weak, passive, or negative. On the other hand, the masculine is energetic and direct. This doesn't mean that it's better than the feminine; it's just what it is.

A better alternative to describe the feminine trait is to say that all feminine signs demonstrate a quiet strength in being self-contained and possessing inner resolve, while the masculine signs display their powers through outwardly directed action.

The masculine types are Aquarius, Libra, Aries, Leo, Gemini, and Sagittarius, while the feminine types are the Taurus, Pisces, Cancer, Capricorn, Scorpio, and last but not least, Virgo.

Triplicities

We can also split the twelve zodiac signs into groups of four, with three signs to each group. These groups are called triplicities, and they each represent one of the four components: Earth, Air, Water, and Fire. These elements make up the basic characteristics of the twelve types.

Earth signs — Virgo, Capricorn, and Taurus — are stable and practical thinkers. Air signs — Libra, Gemini, and Aquarius — are communicative and intellectual. Water signs — Cancer, Pisces, and Scorpio — are in touch with their intuition and emotions. Finally, the Fire signs — Leo, Aries, and Sagittarius — are enthusiastic and often active.

Quadruplicities

We also split all zodiac signs into three groups of four, known as quadruplicities, all of which signify particular traits. There are three qualities in particular:

- Cardinal
- Fixed
- Mutable

The cardinal signs are regularly the most outgoing and enterprising of the lot. They're the ones who start things. If you want someone who is an innate initiator, you can turn to the Capricorn, Cancer, Libra, and Aries signs.

The fixed signs are Scorpio, Leo, Aquarius, and Taurus. They're not open to change, which can be good since they finish and perfect what they start, rather than initiate things.

Mutable signs are Virgo, Gemini, Pisces, and Sagittarius. They're versatile, quick to adapt, and flexible. They're open and able to adjust depending on the circumstances they're facing.

The thought to remember that there's no zodiac sign with the exact combination of elements, dualities, and qualities. Thanks to the unique combos, all signs naturally express themselves differently from one another.

Polarities

This is the final grouping of zodiac signs, where two signs are assigned to a group. We call each grouping a polarity, meaning to comprise opposing signs with conflicting natures. Let's quickly look at the polarities:

- Where Sagittarius is all about philosophy and higher mental activities, Gemini is all about self-expression.

- Aquarius is all about large-scale ideals and hopes, while Leo is about creativity and personal pleasure.

- Libra is focused on partnership, while Aries is about individuality.

- Capricorn is a sign that's about public life, while Cancer is about life at home.

- Scorpio is about shared possessions and building legacies, while Taurus is about their personal possessions.

- Pisces are all self-delusion and dreams, while Virgo is about self-advancement and function.

Each sign of the zodiac has its lucky days and numbers, special colors and plants, jewels, metals, places, and so on. They too, have their positive attributes and their challenges. I'm not suggesting you live your life by this. As a Virgo, you're more than welcome to wear other colors besides Virgo colors, and to try playing the lottery on any day of the week besides your lucky one; it wouldn't mean the end of the world. However, you might find it fascinating to try experimenting with what you're about to learn. Since this book is all about the Virgo, we shall now turn our attention to just this amazing sign.

The Virgo (August 22 — September 22)

Here's a quick guide on all you need to know about being a Virgo.

- Your duality is feminine.

- Your triplicity or element is Earth.

- Your quality or quadruplicity is mutable. You are discriminating, practical, modest, and reserved. You're an industrious person with a piercing analytical mind, willing to painstakingly seek knowledge and understanding in all you do.

- Your ruling planet is Mercury. This is the ancient god of commerce and communication. This planet oversees reason and intelligence and predisposes you to be a bit high strung or "mercurial."

- Your symbol is The Virgin. The Virgin represents pure motives, industriousness, modesty, and service. You use your talents to help other people. The typical depiction of the Virgin has her holding a sheaf of wheat. This sheaf represents you using your skills, knowledge, and ideas to the benefit (or nourishment) of everyone in the world.

- Your glyph (a written symbol) represents the Virgin because it is the pictorial representation of the human sexual organs, untouched and without blemish. Your glyph has two curved lines (one crossed) and a straight line. This signifies the way you interweave emotions and feelings with wisdom and practicality.

- Your dominant key phrase is *I Analyze.*

- Your polarity is the Pisces. Where the Pisces is about self-deception and buying into illusions, the Virgo is about responsibility and personal-improvement. Where the Piscean revels in imagination, dreaminess, self-delusion, escapism, and vagueness, the Virgo is quite practical and grounded.

• The body parts ruled by the Virgo include the intestines and the nervous system. As a Virgo, you're quite susceptible to illnesses caused by nervous tension and stress. Ulcers are a common concern with you.

• Your lucky day is Wednesday.

• Your lucky numbers are 3 and 5.

• Your magical birthstone is Sapphire, which gives you peace and tranquility of mind, and keeps you safe against injury and illness as you travel.

• Your special colors are Gray and Navy Blue, which both signify a refined taste.

• Your cities include Paris, Heidelberg, Boston, and Strasbourg.

• Your countries are Greece, Turkey, West Indies, and Crete.

• Your flowers are the pansy and morning glory.

• Your trees are nut-bearing trees.

• Your metal is Mercury.

• Your animals are small, domesticated pets.

• Your challenge: As a Virgo, you can't help but interfere, offer criticism, and appear unemotional. These features can make others get angry and violent, so you want to be aware of that.

A-List of Famous Virgos

1. Beyoncé

2. Zendaya

3. Idris Elba

4. Taraji P. Henson

5. Salma Hayek

6. Keanu Reeves

7. Lili Reinhart

8. Keke Palmer

The Virgo at Work

You'd be hard-pressed to find any better boss or employee than a Virgo. You work really hard, and you're intelligent, an undeniable asset. When people need to get jobs done, you're the best woman or man for the job.

One of your strongest traits is your attention to details — even the incredibly small stuff that most individuals won't notice. You're not the kind to be sloppy. You'll be damned before you pass off something that's even remotely incomplete as finished.

You're careful about the decisions you make, and you have a precise process for getting things done. Sometimes your particular work process and awareness to detail make it hard for the others you work with, since most of them would rather move things along as fast as they can. But you are not willing to sacrifice quality for speed, and so you're comfortable getting everyone to take a moment and go through the project at hand with a magnifying glass so you can work all the kinks out. As a result, perfection is something you tend to achieve.

At the office, you're analytical, practical, hardworking, loyal, and gentle. These are your strengths. Alternatively, you are critical of yourself, wondering if you delivered your best and if you shouldn't perhaps try to do more.

You're critical of others, too, because you can't stand it when people don't do what they should do properly, and you don't understand how anyone could be so sloppy. You're not critical because you enjoy being difficult, but because nothing pleases you more than being able to deliver flawless execution on a project.

Sometimes you worry a lot about what could go wrong, and often will not rest until you get feedback that says you did well. Also, you are a tad shy — and you can overcome this by simply voicing your thoughts. You are, after all, more intelligent than most.

As a Virgo at work, you are a hard worker, and you solve problems. You're amazing to work with, especially when you allow yourself to be generous and kind. No matter the job, you're an invaluable asset to the team, always.

The Virgo at a Party

Virgos and parties are a tricky thing. Now and then, you'll let your hair down and have fun, but usually, that's only after a few drinks have loosened you up. This doesn't mean you're not social; you'd rather hang out with people one-on-one or in small groups.

You're probably the person who sits at the party with a drink, enjoying watching other people dancing and being goofy. It's not that you're a party pooper, and it's not that you're not having a good time. You just love to observe.

When you do get in on the "madness," you have a great time! You leave everyone's jaw hanging, whether it's you belting out the tunes to a Christina Aguilera song with particularly high notes, or dancing like the love child of Ciara and the late great Michael Jackson.

But, when the alcohol wears off, you are more than happy to take a seat — or leave. One thing you could never be accused of is being that *one friend* who doesn't know when the party's over. Speaking of firewater, when you notice you've had way more than you should have, you're the first one to head right home. You have incredible self-control and will only let yourself sway from side to side and crumble into a puddle on the floor when you're in the relative safety of your home or with people you love and trust.

The Virgo at Home

As a Virgo, nothing matters to you more than a home that is neat and tidy. You may not be religious, but you definitely take the phrase "Cleanliness is next to godliness" to heart. You live by it. Your home must be in order. You care little for clutter and will declutter often and regularly. You've probably had your friends and family raise eyebrows at you when you say stuff like, "I need to clear this place out," because from where they're standing, there's nothing that needs clearing!

You love it when your home has lots of space and lots of light. So, creating this space, you live and breathe the idea that everything has its space. It's not just that you're stubborn about this need for an order for nothing; it's that you really need the order to function. Without it, you can't help feeling off and not at peace.

With home decor, you choose minimalism. This doesn't mean a lack of taste by any stretch of the imagination. You pay attention to color, style, materials, craftsmanship, and every other element in every room of your home. You love to have beautiful items that increase your home's elegance but are also functional and practical.

If anyone wants to get to know you, they'll find the real you in the comfort of your home. Where outside, you might be accused of being a tad too straightlaced and having resting rhymes-with-witch face, at home, you let loose totally. You might break into a silly song and dance routine just because you're about to have an amazing pizza, or, well, *just because.*

Since the home is where you are okay with being vulnerable, you are mindful of who you let into your space. Even when they're with you, you're mindful of how long they stay there — unless they're part of those you consider near and dear.

Chapter Two: Virgo Strengths and Weaknesses

In this chapter, we will take a quick look at the Virgo's strengths and weaknesses when they are a friend or family member. So, let's begin!

The Virgo's Strengths

Of all the traits you or your friend have as a Virgo, the most admirable one is conscientiousness. You make a point of doing a good job at whatever responsibility has been assigned to you, and inevitably this leads you to greener pastures and higher ranks, whatever your field is.

As enigmatic as you seem, the real action goes on beneath your calm, cool exterior. Inside, you're restless, eager to be making the most of your time. You're intense in a controlled and focused way, and you direct that intensity to things you think will improve your life.

You're really not the kind to just binge on Netflix all day in your pajamas, and chances are on the rare occasions you do give in to that urge, you're still going to make sure you at least did one thing you saw as productive before you hit the hay. As far as you're concerned, there's always a chance to be better and do better, and you snatch every second to work on being a better version of yourself.

It's not a random turn of events that you're so obsessed with needing to do stuff. After all, your ruling planet is Mercury! That means you love the constant activity, whether it's learning to become a stock trader or figuring out how to become a better gardener. You are driven to make things happen and make them happen as perfectly as possible.

The Virgo absolutely sucks at procrastinating. You're incredibly organized most of the time, and you're all about making things happen. While the rest of the world dreams, you do.

As a Virgo, you are open to love, but you need a lot more than love to be happy and at peace with yourself. For you, it's not enough to have a lover, or friends, or kids, or a home. You want to be sure that you mean something; that your existence is contributing to bettering the whole.

You are full of ambition, and for you, it's not just about raking in dollars. It's about wanting to grow in knowledge and wisdom and to apply all that you've learned in a way that benefits you and everyone around you.

No one has as pure a purpose as you do. In fact, this is the thing that the Virgo stands for. You're not living your life to exploit people. You aspire to much higher ideals, and nothing appeals to you more than the chance to be of service.

Long ago, Virgo symbolized the harvest. Recall the image of the Virgin, with a sheaf of wheat in her hand? This represents that those under the Sun sign Virgo will always take the skills, knowledge, wisdom, and information they have, plant it, and then harvest the fruits to enjoy and share the benefits of all that they have sown. You, dear Virgo, are a nourisher.

If there's one thing no one can accuse you of, it's not being unintelligent. Your memory is sharp, your mind crisp and capable of analyzing as no one else can, and you can cut through the haze and arrive at clear answers thanks to your mental faculties.

Another thing you're incredibly great at is figuring out why people really do what they do, no matter what they claim their reasons are. You are most likely the one your friends and family check-in with before they do major or important stuff because you are often great at fishing out the weak links in their plans.

Logic is your playground, so you have no issues with ripping apart a problem and reconstructing it into its solution. You're excellent at coming up with answers and putting an end to disagreements.

It's not like you to make a decision before you have all the facts that you need. You thrive in the world of facts and turn your nose up at such things as psychics and crystal balls and whatnot. You're not swift to make judgments based on emotions, and you don't particularly like it when people do that either.

The Virgo's Weaknesses and How to Navigate Them

As great as always being rational is, consider making room for such concepts as faith, spirituality, and synchronicity. Since you are a fact loving Virgo, here's a fact you will definitely love more and more while you ponder it: Things happen and we meet people for a reason. It's not random. This is the challenge you face as a Virgo: To be willing to accept and allow for such things as faith.

Your ruling planet Mercury is all about thought and assumptions, and these things are what form the reality you experience. To assume the worst and always think the worst will inevitably lead to the worst experiences for you.

You need to know your tendency to avoid your true emotions because you'd rather indulge in denial. You might insist you're not mad at something, or that you're all right with the way things have turned out when someone else gets the guy or the girl or gets the cushy job or promotion you wanted. All this does is keep the ugly feelings hidden within you.

Another thing you want to be mindful of is your tendency to be focused on one thing to the exclusion of the big picture. You have amazing talent in organization and being precise, but sometimes that makes it hard to notice if anything else that matters is going on.

Because you trust logic explicitly, it makes it hard for you to be imaginative, and inspiration doesn't strike you as often as you could let it. You tend to fall back on what you already know works, rather than look to the new. It matters to you to learn why things work the way they do and how they work. The good thing is you're a mutable Sun sign, so you can make changes as needed so you can incorporate the new into the old.

You might make too much of a habit of turning molehills into mountains. You take a small, simple problem and blow it out of proportion by complicating it. What you might want to learn to do is not be so analytical of things; sometimes things really are as they seem, and there's nothing more to them than that.

As a Virgo, you're naturally reserved, maybe even a little shy. You don't make small talk a habit as it's anything but relaxing for you to shoot the breeze with strangers about such mundane things as the weather or your choice in nail polish. You'd rather deal with people on deeper things that actually matter; it is in this situation where you thrive, and your laser-like wits and intellect shine through. In your one-on-one interactions, you allow people to see just how full of wit, insight, charm, perception, and wisdom you are.

You don't kid yourself by saying, "Money doesn't matter." You know of its importance, and you're an expert at handling your finances, even if you don't like to toot your own horn. You're not the kind to shell out money on needless things or snake oil. This doesn't mean that you're a cheapskate; you're just adept at getting incredible value for a steal.

Because you're very clear about what you accept and don't accept, you can get just a tad too critical. You're not okay with the status quo, and you'll do all you can to make things better. You'll push people to give better than their best.

Sometimes, because you're so aware of all the ways things could be better, you let this knowledge get the best of you, and you get unhappy. However, you do the best you can to avoid being in situations where others can criticize what you're doing wrong – unless you're the unique kind of Virgo who can handle criticism and is okay with admitting they don't always get it right.

As far as your health goes, you want nothing short of the best for yourself. You never need a call from your doctor asking you to come in for a checkup because you show up all on your own, like clockwork. You take your vitamins, and you move your body as often and as well as you can. This is great, but you need to beware of your tendency to worry too much about your health. When you worry like this, you become tense and nervous, which naturally predisposes you to fall ill. Also, be mindful of giving in to hypochondria, where you assume you're sick even though you're fine.

There's nothing as amazing as being in the right relationship, where there is much warmth and love. You're a naturally loving, giving, loyal, devoted, and kind soul, being born under the Sun sign of Virgo. Whenever someone is fortunate enough to win your love, you do all that you can to serve them and keep them happy.

Who You Really Are

There's no one as dedicated and strong-willed as you are, and you'll go to any lengths to make sure you see something through to the end, and it's all perfect. The reason you're this way is simple: You can't stand the thought of being a failure at something, and you lean toward being a little too hard on yourself. As "critical" as people think you are, you dial your criticism up to the hundreds when you aim it at yourself.

If anyone thinks they can figure you out, they need to think again. You're a puzzle, bound up in mystery, shrouded in an enigma. When you're dealing with people you don't know too well; you'll often hold back. Even those you know and love will still describe you as reserved. As cool as you seem on the outside, there's a gushing torrent of emotions on the inside where no one else can see. No one is as intense as the Virgo, and not only that, but you are also given to sensitivity at extreme levels — something no one you don't want to know will ever know about.

You enjoy being able to take care of people around you, whether that means providing materially or giving much needed useful advice. However, you like when you're shown appreciation for your acts. It matters to you that the people you help actively demonstrate that you're not wasting your time and that they are thankful for what you offer them. For you, it matters that you serve a purpose, that you provide assistance because people do matter to you.

Who Others See You As

People think of you as someone who is an achiever. You are the epitome of the go-getter. As such, you're often assigned a lot of responsibility, and people trust you to handle whatever they throw your way. They know that you can deal with any problem you face because of your incomparable skills.

Your friends and family will often come to you so you can help them understand why they act the way they do, or why they feel how they do about their career, loved ones, or whatever else is bothering them.

You are incredibly skilled at prioritizing and finding the order in the midst of the madness. Where everyone is losing their heads, you're the one keeping things rock steady.

Because you're picky (in a good way), people will always look at your recommendations on everything from cuisine, to fashion, to books and movies. You never, ever let anyone in so easily. Your heart may be *wherever*, but it is most definitely never going to be on your sleeve. For this reason, some people erroneously assume that you're cold and unfeeling. If only they knew just how deeply you feel for and care about them!

The Virgo in the Family

If you could change the way a few of your relatives acted, would you do it? Be honest. Think about that one creepy uncle, or that nitpicking sibling, or your overbearing mum. Sometimes we wish we could change the people fate threw us with, but since we don't have a wand or a magic spell to fix them, the only other choice we have left is to run away... Okay, that may be a tad dramatic. Perhaps we could try understanding them a little better instead. This is where astrology can prove quite helpful! Looking at the stars, you can figure out what exactly makes the Virgo tick.

With astrology, you must consider other things besides the Zodiac signs and where they're placed, as these things also play an important function in your unique family dynamics. I'm referring to the modalities we spoke about earlier — mutable, cardinal, and fixed — and the elements — Earth, fire, water, and air.

The Virgo belongs to the Earth element, so you'll find them having qualities reminiscent of Earth. For one thing, you'll find that they're the most down-to-Earth family member of yours. They're modest about the things they've accomplished and are capable of, and they're also incredibly grounded.

Virgo is the most pragmatic person you know at home. You'll notice that they can be a wee bit conservative sometimes, and that's okay. They love to have a routine, as it gives them a sense of order and stability, and makes them feel safe and at ease.

You'll notice your Virgo relative loves to analyze things and makes a point of being practical, thinking through every angle before they make a decision or a move. The thing about Earth: it is *rock steady*, unlike air and fire. The Virgo is not a big fan of surprises. A surefire way to incur their wrath or make them feel uncomfortable would be to put them on the spot. But ... if the Virgo has learned to embrace her mutable trait, then she will handle whatever you throw at her — while letting you know after your little stunt that what you did was not cool with her!

Just like it's not so easy to change a rock into something else, the Virgo is not entirely open to change. They're an organized lot, you see, and they'd rather do something they're familiar and comfortable with than risk rocking the boat. This might seem like a terrible thing, but it isn't. You'll find that the calmest, most patient, and most steadfast head at home is the Virgo. You can rely on them to get the job done. You can trust that if they said they're going to start doing something, it's going to get done.

In the midst of confusion, panic, or a heated argument, you can draw upon your Virgo relative's infinite well of reason. The next time there's a crisis, look around the room, and you'll notice that the Virgo is the most poised person there. The only problem with them being so steadfast, poised, and stable is that you might find it hard to tell what they're feeling or thinking. Not that this is a problem. If you want to know what's running around in their heads, just ask. Don't be pushy about it; in their own time and in their own way, they will give you an answer.

Earth is an element all about materialism. This doesn't mean your Virgo relative is materialistic by any stretch of the imagination — at least, not in a superficial way. Do they have high sophistication in taste? They do. But they're not big on an ostentatious display of their possessions, or anyone else's, for that matter.

For the Virgo, what matters the most is emotional dependability and stability. They find that just as important as being on a financial stable ground. Speaking of money, the Virgo does their best to make sure it's never a problem so they can live life without ever having to worry about cash.

Another interesting thing about this Earth sign is that they love to touch, and they have sensuality in spades. You might not think them all sugar and spice and everything nice, but they're affectionate, sentimental, and genuine in all their feelings.

Earth Meets Water

If you consider nature, you'll notice that water and Earth have a relationship that benefits each other. This is the same thing with the Earth Virgo and any other water signs in the family. If you're a water sign yourself, and you have a Virgo relative, you've probably noticed that you have good vibes with each other. Earth and water bind, deeply, unshakably, and effortlessly.

Being of the Earth, the Virgo has all the patience they need to deal with the complex nature and moods of water signs. At the same time, Water signs are great at emotionally supporting the Virgo and creating a comfortable and safe space for the Virgo to get into their feelings. Sure, the Pisces might think of the Virgo as being wound up too tight, but there's really nothing but love there. The Water sign will often push the Virgo to be a lot more compassionate and perceptive emotionally, while the Earth will give Water calm and stability.

Earth Meets Air

The Virgo and air signs all share a similar sense of humor: Droll. They have the same sensibilities as well: Delicate. And what about their views on drama? Distasteful. That being said, because of the Virgo's practical nature, they might have a problem with how frenetic and unpredictable air signs tend to be. On the flip side, if you're an Air sign, you probably think the Virgo is just unyielding, way too rigid, and too darned measured in every step they take.

While the air sign is all about ideas, the Virgo, being of the Earth, prefers the tangible and practical. If you're the parent of a Virgo and a Libra, for instance, don't be upset by your child taking issue with you when you're indecisive. Don't despair, though; your Virgo can teach you why it's worth it to commit to a decision, and you can teach them how to let loose and be a little more spontaneous.

Earth Meets Fire

You'd be hard-pressed to find more opposite elements... Okay, there's fire and water, but we're talking about the Virgo here. Fire signs tend to be spontaneous, and this is the opposite of the cautious Virgo. If you're a Virgo parent, this is the reason your Sagittarius kid finds you a little too stifling. That doesn't mean there's no upside to this tricky dance between Earth and Fire.

Virgo could stand to gain a lot from the fire sign's love for life and living, learning to be okay with experiencing the new or unfamiliar and making peace with the unknown. On the flip side, the Virgo can help their fire sign relatives by giving them stable footing and teaching the value of focus, consistency, and patience.

The Mutable Virgo in the Family

Since the Virgo is mutable, that means they're incredibly flexible and versatile; they can learn to deal with change. Almost like a chameleon, they adjust to whatever environment or situation they find themselves in.

No one is as accommodating, compromising, and obliging as the mutable Virgo. Ironically, as organized and practical as the Virgo is, and as deeply in love as they are with their routines, they'll go with the flow whenever the circumstances dictate they should.

The mutable Virgo deliberately takes the least resistant path. They're the best team player you could have. They're not keen on leading, but they can light the path when it comes to teaching the rest of the family to be at peace with new developments and be willing to settle in.

Being mutable means the Virgo is not a fan of conflict in the family. They will do their best to see things from everyone's perspectives, and it's this quality of theirs that makes them excellent mediators, helping people sort out their differences and getting things back to normal.

Chapter Three: The Virgo Child

The Virgo baby is a sensitive and touching child. They get startled by all sounds, prefer to be touched only by familiar people, and cry when a voice around them doesn't sound tender enough.

The Virgo babies distinguish between strangers and family early in life, and they are uncomfortable with being left alone with unfamiliar faces. They are prone to restlessness caused by uncomfortable cribs, sharp sounds, wet diapers, and bright light.

While the Virgo baby won't cry severely, they will surely throw tantrums. They will whimper and keep their faces wrinkled until their comfort is restored. These guys need a constant stream of love and encouragement; otherwise, they feel helpless and unprotected.

Virgo children lean toward dealing with insecurities even at that young age, and this keeps them from participating in children's groups and any unfamiliar event or communicating with strangers. But don't be fooled; they are self-confident and fearless little ones, but only in the company of loving, familiar faces.

Virgo children are typically curious about their surrounding space and are attracted to everything unknown despite being hesitant and cautious. They will never jump headfirst into a strange situation, and no steps will be taken without the guidance of a familiar adult. Even then, they will continually look to the adult for approval or reaction while moving ahead. The adult is tasked to supply praise, self-confidence, and explanations.

The minute they learn to speak, everything speeds up! Virgo babies will ask about anything and everything, especially the names of things. They seem to have a knack for that. Reading becomes one of their favorite things to do. They recall all the poems and stories, repeating them happily as often as they feel the need to.

They prefer completely harmless toys like dolls, cubes, or teddy bears. They are also enthusiastic about plot games, taking on the role of doctor, teacher, parent, and so on. These little ones are completely taken with animals and will deeply appreciate owning a pet like a puppy, parrot, hamster, kitten, and so on. This helps them develop discipline and a sense of responsibility early in life because they are quick to figure out how to take care of their tiny animal friend.

The minute they can move around comfortably, little Virgos become great helpers. They will jump at opportunities to participate in chores around the house like washing dishes, cleaning the floor, or at least trying to, especially when they receive any praise and encouragement. This habit sticks because they quickly learn to clean up their toys, stay neat, and ensure that their rooms are in order as best as they can for a little human. Mostly, this behavior extends well into adulthood, especially if they received praise and encouragement from their parents or guardians during the formative years.

As a preschooler, they might prefer to spend most of their time playing alone, drawing or figuring out their toys. For learning, the Virgo preschooler commits! But often, there is one thing that causes problems for these kids: communication with fellow children. This can go unnoticed until it is time to play team sports or any activity that involves teamwork.

Virgo children are usually found alone, preferring to observe and engage from a distance. Without guidance from parents or teachers, they might become so isolated that they begin to think they are not like others, sometimes leading to an inferiority complex.

As I mentioned earlier, Virgo children place a lot of importance on neatness. They must maintain that purity internally and externally. They are trustworthy, especially with finances, being the kind to spend their school money on meals or anything that seems practical and useful. They are eerily calm, making one wonder what goes on in their tiny heads.

Expressing emotion doesn't come easily to them because of their intense levels of restraint and quietness. Everything they say is thoroughly thought through more times than you can imagine. This is a double-edged sword as it can be a blessing to have a calm and collected child or a problem when you need to know what issues they might be going through.

The Male Virgo Child

All Virgos are deep thinkers. The Earth is a grounding force for those born under this sign, unlike the daredevils of the fire signs. This is the reason the young male Virgo is drawn more to mental activities than the physical ones. The Virgo boy thinks through as many possibilities as he can and plan for each one. If you have a Virgo boy, you've likely noticed how infrequently you need to remind him to take caution because he always does! He isn't prone to the use of brute force, militancy, or bravado. Instead, he leans towards attentiveness, foresight, and intelligence.

This does not mean that every little detail in the Virgo boy's mind is placed in compartments. There are moments when he experiences anxiety – even when he shouldn't. This is the price to pay for constantly absorbing information, as knowledge can prevent one from acting without a care in the world.

For instance, he may be excessively concerned about little things and hold himself back from experiences he would have otherwise enjoyed had he not been riddled with worry.

The Virgo boy does not like compromises. This can annoy others who don't see through the Virgo lens, which enhances the content and standard of everything around. A Virgo boy can easily be perceived as picky and petty when, in reality, he is just observant and alert.

The Female Virgo Child

The little girls in this category possess a strong wish to know and understand things in life. Where they're not nurtured in a warm, loving environment, this desire to understand everything can morph into an ugly need to manipulate — which isn't their fault if they aren't raised by the best of parents.

Keen observation and the ability to choose are characteristic of the Virgo girl at an early age. She's a good communicator and an even better listener. During her moments of silence, her eyes constantly see the world, noting the words and actions of those around her. She'll spend a lot of time analyzing the world around her in her head.

Because the Virgo girl requires perfection, she is prone to an inferiority complex. Outside of the right support systems, she can be her own worst critic because she creates unrealistic expectations of herself in her head. These expectations make her wrongly assume that she will never be enough as she is. This is why she needs a proper foundation of love and care, and would stand to gain a lot from being with people who *do* see her efforts and acknowledge them while letting her know she's fine just as she is. Most important, she needs to know that it is okay to make mistakes. This is especially important because the less she sets impossible standards for herself, the more she'll be able to enjoy a rich, fulfilling life.

The Virgo girl's inner voice tells her to do her best to make a good impression on the surrounding people. This can be a good or bad thing. This is a great thing sometimes because it means she'll make sure that she can connect with the people around her and create a comfortable space for one and all.

On the flip side, it could mean she gets bent all out of shape because she's trying to adhere to other people's standards for her life while neglecting her own joy — and some of those standards are actually based on her assumptions of what she thinks is required of her, not what the others in her life explicitly ask for.

Health of the Virgo Child

The intestines and stomach are the Virgo child's vulnerabilities, and they can be particularly prone to poisoning. You need to be careful when selecting meals for the Virgo baby. Just because something works great for other babies doesn't mean it's just as good for your Virgo child.

Remember that your Virgo child is susceptible to nervous disorders, and they tend to withhold their emotions from people they do not trust. Even when you — their loving and trusted parent — need to know how they're feeling, let them understand they can let you know anything, and be sure not to condemn or judge them for what they feel.

Virgo children tend to develop lung disease, but gastrointestinal problems are more common. Don't worry if your Virgo child is skinny growing up. Whatever you do, don't force-feed them! Their digestive system is finely tuned, and they're in touch with it. If they don't wish to eat something, or they don't want to eat anymore, trust that it's for a good reason — even if they don't know the fancy medical jargon to explain it to you. If you're worried that they don't have enough of an appetite, you can always consult with your medical doctor rather than take matters into your own hands.

Virgos eat the exact food that they need, and if that means they are a little smaller than the other kids, no problem. They have great intuition for selecting what works for them and what doesn't. This isn't synonymous with ignoring your Virgo child if they are underweight, so get help if that is the case.

Hobbies of the Virgo Child

One of the first things you'll notice about a Virgo child is that they tend to finish whatever they start. They are overly self-critical and can spot their own shortcomings and mistakes before you do, so don't bother pointing them out.

The Virgo child already knows where they went wrong with whatever they're doing. If you think you're offering assistance by showing them their mistakes, you're not. You will only completely demoralize them. They thrive in intense concentration, so don't be surprised if they throw a fit because you invaded their personal space to offer your "recommendations."

The Virgo child is drawn to any activity that requires intense concentration. They love to read, write, draw, paint, play instruments, or do whatever else they can with their hands if they're so inclined. They have an incredible eye for detail, so you can expect that whatever they're doing will be hands-down amazing.

Whatever your Virgo child is attracted to, you can count on one thing: they will be deeply focused on it. Sometimes, you might struggle to get them to drop what they're doing to come and have a bath or dinner. Don't take this to heart and don't force them to leave either. Just let them know they have a few more minutes to wrap up, and then they can come back to their hobby when they're done taking care of their tummies or bodies.

The Virgo Child at School

Virgo children are almost always the ideal student at school. They have a lot of fun learning, which is the whole point of school, anyway. They love books, be they full of stories or intriguing concepts about life. Your Virgo will never be one to cheat in exams. Often, the other kids want to cheat off of them. They're the students you'll see scribbling away and probably needing an extra sheet because they want to get down every thought they have about what they've learned so far.

Parental Advice

Show your Virgo child as much as you can of the world through books, travel, documentaries, or whatever. This is important because it opens them up to the possible ways they can express themselves. You'll be taking advantage of the mutability of their sign by allowing them to have an array of different ways they can structure their life.

Do not try even for a second to insinuate that there's anything wrong with your child's need for order and structure. Encourage them! But as you do, let them know that not everyone is as neat and orderly as they are, that it's okay, and that they can be accommodating of other people's messes within reason.

When you need to offer criticism to your Virgo child, you must make sure it is constructive, meaning you build them up rather than tear them down. Share your criticisms with them as a friend. Use persuasion and influence, not punishments and force. Rather than say, "You should have done it this way," encourage them to come around to your way of thinking by asking, "What if you tried it this way? What do you think about that?" If they offer you reasons, they don't think it could work, then gently coax them by asking, "Well, what else do you think we could try doing that might be even better than what we did before?"

You never need to raise your voice at your Virgo kid to make a point, because they actually are logical and get you anyway. Yelling does only makes them clam up and make sure you'll never learn what they think or feel about anything ever again. Your Virgo child doesn't care for violence, anger, or confrontation — especially when they're the recipient.

Give them access to books - *many* books - be they storybooks, encyclopedias, travel books, etc. It is from these books that the child can form their own world view. This doesn't mean your child doesn't care for toys and gadgets, so please get them those as well. Whatever hobbies they have, it is your job as their parent to create an environment that allows them to engage in them as passionately as their little hearts want to.

Just as important as letting your Virgo child explore her natural proclivities is helping them learn how to interact with others and come out of their shell. Show her it's okay to work with others by having her join children in groups — preferably ones centered on her interests. When she becomes okay with the concept of spending time with others, she'll be open to exploring activities outside her comfort zone, knowing she now has the tools to interact with others around her.

The Virgo child drifts away from his parents or guardians if he feels misunderstood, so it is important to build and cement the trust between you two in the child's formative years. Talk to him with an air of calmness, without judgment or reproach. Genuinely be happy with and for him.

Chapter Four: Virgo and Love

Here's an interesting fact about Virgos: They tend to take extra time falling in love. It's not that they're incapable of love, or not given to being all dreamy and romantic, but for them, whoever they will give their heart to has got to be worth it.

The Virgo does not care for silly, meaningless flings; they want depth, they want the truth, and they want dependability. No matter how many butterflies they feel in their stomach when you pass by or when they smell something that reminds them of you, they'll still keep their heart firmly where it belongs unless (and until) they can be certain you are here for the long haul.

The Virgo: The True Sapiosexual

Virgos are the sexy nerds of the zodiac. As a Virgo, you consider the mind the sexiest aspect of a person. You're a sucker for amazing conversations, witty banter, and even double entendres. There's nothing you love more than conversation tennis, where the other person can give back as good as they get.

For you, a surefire way for someone on Tinder to go from matched to unmatched in .0000001 milliseconds is when they only ever throw you one-liners... or even worse, one-word replies where they can't even be bothered to spell it all out!

The Virgo: Anything BUT Cold

If you're a Virgo, and you've ever read a book or article that says something to the effect of "Virgos can come off as a tad too cold," then you've probably kicked and screamed against that a million and one times because you know it's not true. Sure, you seem that way sometimes, but usually only with strangers, people you're not comfortable with yet, or people who crossed you.

For being in an intimate relationship, whoever is lucky enough to have you had better be well prepared for the white-hot heat that is your love. When you're sure about someone, you give them yourself one hundred percent. You let them in. You let them dive deep, and there they can see your emotions run deep and true.

Support for Your Virgo

Virgos are their own worst critics, valuing perfection in themselves above all else. Having a partner who showers you with unconditional love, support, and encouragement leads to a healthier and happier Virgo. People should tread carefully and softly with you during conflicts, or they might risk weakening the bond instead of strengthening it.

The Virgo prefers a mature partner, and for a good reason. You need a partner who can be trusted not to overreact to every little crisis, one who can stay focused on the facts of whatever issue you're dealing with in the now, rather than hear only what they want to hear and dredge up irrelevant things.

Best Matches for Virgo

Let's consider the signs that make the best matches for the Virgo. These are signs that bring out the best qualities of the Virgo and can provide a balance for the not-so-great qualities.

Scorpio

The Virgo and The Scorpio are the most amazing match –one of the strongest pairings in the Zodiac. The Scorpio is wild and intense, while the Virgo is down-to-earth, and this makes them work beautifully together.

You both care. A lot. The Scorpio can always be trusted, and they value trust as one of the most important things in any relationship. They're not the best at opening up, but as soon as you work your way into their hearts, they are more than happy to love you with an intensity you could never have imagined possible.

The Virgo is about taking care of other people's needs before they consider themselves, and so often they criticize themselves for not giving even much more than they already do — which is funny because the Virgo gives and gives and gives. As a Virgo, it just feels good to be giving.

Now, you and the Scorpio feel things deeply. Your Scorpio might not be obvious about it, but they're emotional. They'll put up a huge wall so that no one sees that, and they can stay safe. That's right... your Scorpio worries about being vulnerable, so they stay sealed until someone worthy (that's you, Virgo) comes around and breaks them open.

When the Virgo and the Scorpio get together, sparks fly. Things get intense and deep. You each know you can depend on each other. Even as friends, your loyalty knows no limits. You both learn from each other and grow together. The depth of understanding you both share needs no words — not even for you, dear Virgo. You know your

Scorpio through and through, and you're unafraid to be just as naked with them in your heart.

Capricorn

Capricorn makes an amazing partner for Virgo. Being both Earth signs, you are both realistic and prefer to be focused on worldly materials. You both excel in various fields and possess a deep intuition about each other's needs. If a Capricorn-Virgo couple is spotted, they probably met at a work-related occasion and hit it off immediately.

You two have a great sense of humor that keeps you constantly laughing together. It is a good way for you two to relax and unwind, especially to get into a sensuous mood.

Despite all the similarities, you both have distinct traits that allow a balance in your relationship. The Capricorn is usually drowning in work, with their eyes zeroed in on the future, can tend to neglect their health and other important factors in life.

But the Virgo is more focused on the details than any other zodiac sign; still, they are prone to losing focus and getting off track. As a Virgo, you can make sure that your Capricorn lover remembers important details like self-care while your Capricorn can help you maintain focus.

Taurus

This is another wonderful match for you. You are both Earth signs, so you are bound to share the same realistic views of the world. The Taurus is one of the domestic signs of the zodiac while you are the most organized. These qualities are the highlight of your successful relationship.

Like Capricorn, you two also have notable differences that enable you to balance each other. The Taurus is chill and likes to enjoy the pleasures of living. You have no choice but to relax and savor the pleasures of life with them. The Taurus can also be the anchor you need to feel grounded. What you bring to the table as a Virgo is a motivation, among other things.

The Taurus' calmness can easily transition into overindulgence and laziness. You will make sure that Taurus does what needs to be done when it needs to be done, or even sooner because that's just who you are.

Cancer

The Cancer might seem like an odd match for you as a Virgo, but you two score high on the compatibility chart. You deeply understand each other in ways that other signs do not. You also tend to worry and fuss about everything, and this can be annoying to other signs. This similarity fosters tolerance in the relationship because you both get it!

This difference, though, is that despite your tendency to fuss over everything, you fuss about different things. Your perfectionist nature makes you worry about the little imperfections. The nurturing nature of Cancer makes them worry about the needs and safety of others. Cancer is a water sign, so their imagination is as boundless as the ocean. This causes them to exaggerate the threat before them or its potential, making them worry when they don't even need to.

But your different targets of worry create the perfect balance in your relationship. Cancer will soothe you, letting go of the little imperfections while you can bring clarity to the mind of Cancer in the face of imagined threats. This balance will be reinforced if you ever have children because you make the *best parents.*

Pisces

Pisces is your polar opposite. Theoretically, opposite signs score high on the compatibility chart, but only a few opposites are highly compatible in reality. This match is one of the few.

Opposite signs are expected to be the best partners for each other because opposites equal polarity and polarity brings about balance. The polarity between these two signs can't be explained concretely, but it can be observed in practice. While Pisces is focused on the emotional and spiritual side of things (you know, the bigger picture), you are more concerned about the details, the logical and material side of life.

You are both service-oriented and modest, but this is manifested in different ways. Pisces offers compassion and spiritual support while you offer hands-on assistance. This way, they are a match made in heaven. Pisces works to soothe and calm you while you keep Pisces grounded in the real world.

Worst Matches for Virgo

Time to look at the matches that score low on the compatibility chart. This doesn't mean these signs are terrible people; they simply don't go so well together. *Think of ice-cream and fish.*

Aquarius

As intellectual as Aquarius is, they are one of the worst matches for the equally intellectual Virgo. Despite the intense brainiac energy emanating from you two, you think differently.

You enjoy analysis and practicality, and you like to categorize stuff. Aquarius gets their kicks from thinking *outside* of the box. You both speak different languages, but you have immense intellectual respect for each other even with these differences.

Besides that, there isn't much else going on between you two, especially romantically. To Aquarius, you are overly critical and fussy, while you are constantly annoyed by Aquarius' disregard for rules.

You both don't have a connecting factor or anything to attract you to each other, so it is likely that you will never even consider a relationship with each other. You may end up as work colleagues or just friends interested in a shared hobby.

Leo

Leo also has few common interests with Virgo. Unlike you and Aquarius, where you simply feel nothing for each other, the match between you and Leo will annoy the signs. Ironically, this sometimes works to form a bond between you.

Leo enjoys being the center of positive attention and admiration while you would rather stay backstage working the strings. Leo thinks that you are critical and petty, while you think the Leo is arrogant and pompous.

Like Aquarius and Virgo, it is unlikely for a romantic connection to be established between Leo and Virgo. It is possible for you to go on dates once or twice, but they yield nothing substantial. You are not bad people as individuals; you just don't fit romantically.

Sagittarius

Sagittarius and Virgo are 90 degrees apart on the zodiac wheel. This type of relationship is called a square. Theoretically, this indicates incompatibility, but in reality, square signs form better relationships than signs with no feature at all. The tension produced by their position on the zodiac wheel can bring about a great amount of sexual chemistry between the parties.

Despite the sizzling sexual tension between you two, you are highly incompatible. Things might be blazing in the bedroom, but outside of that, you find it hard to connect or move forward on the same foot.

Physical chemistry and romantic feelings might be enough to attract you, but if the relationship is to survive, the two of you must be able to function together outside of sex.

The problem is, when you even attempt a non-sexual activity together, Sagittarius quickly becomes bored and frustrated with your over-analysis and attention to detail. Meanwhile, you get wracked with anxiety and nervousness over Sagittarius' enthusiasm for cutting corners.

Quick Recap

Romantic compatibility is high with you and Capricorn, Pisces, Taurus, and Cancer. They understand your personality and provide stability and balance to your sign. But your literal match made in heaven is the Scorpio.

You have almost nothing in common with Leo and Aquarius. This lack of a common denominator is the reason for your inability to become romantically involved with one another. There is sizzling sexual tension, but between Sagittarius and you. While this is great, you cannot accomplish any task together outside of sex.

When looking to zodiac compatibility for guidance, always remember that a successful relationship requires much more. Compatibility will tell you which signs are the best together, but the success of a relationship depends also on dedication and commitment. With adequate dedication and commitment, even the most incompatible signs can experience a beautiful relationship. Without these qualities, even the best pairs become incompatible.

As for Virgo, you are a pretty straightforward sign. You are not a player. Think back to your first time at the beach as a kid when you were cautious, testing the water. You took it slowly, didn't you? That was the Virgo in you. You are logical and methodical. You avoid emotional exposure, so you take their time to make sure that the person is worth the emotional risk and effort.

The Teen Virgo and Relationships

It can get difficult to know when a Virgo is developing feelings for you, especially when they haven't crossed that boundary into adulthood just yet. The males have a tendency to always move with a wingman. It's nothing serious; they just like to know that they won't be rejected when they make their move.

The teen takes his time to observe his potential love interest, keeping an eye out for any red flags. When he is completely convinced, he has no problems moving in fast to get the girl.

Virgo teens, in general, are overwhelmed by the newness of love initially, but beneath all that is a lover that is prepared to protect, adore, spoil and lavish you with gifts and attention.

Thinking Long-Term with The Virgo

Every relationship has a honeymoon phase, usually initially – when things are great – and you two seem completely smitten with each other. For some, this phase continues throughout the relationship. For others, things go downhill.

If you're with a Virgo, you might notice them becoming critical of things you do, and becoming even more of a perfectionist. None of this comes from a place of contempt, so don't read it the wrong way. Often, if your Virgo is letting you know things they aren't comfortable with, guess what? The only reason they're doing that is that they've grown to love you that much more. They trust that you'll see what they're saying as coming from a place of wanting you to be the best version of yourself.

To the Virgo, the way you express yourself with these criticisms matters. Speak with your partner as your deepest, truest friend — which, knowing you, they are. You want to be gentle and easy with them.

If you come from a place of love, then each time you and your partner discuss your issues, you'll make progress. Tap into your sensitive side as you speak with them. Put yourself in their shoes and let your words wash over you too. This way, you'll know exactly how to communicate with your lover so it is productive, healthy, and uplifting for you both. While you're at it, hear them out too!

Diving Deep into the Emotions of the Virgo

You are sometimes perceived as an introvert because you don't express your emotions as often or as quickly as other signs. Expressing emotions can seem like a threat to your outward image of calmness and control, so you'd usually rather not indulge — except for when you're in love. You will be emotional because you trust your partner enough to know they will not use that vulnerability against you.

Committing to a Virgo

Signs that are compatible usually hold similar ideals and seek balance in life. Virgos want a romantic partner they will mate to for life, but that rarely happens at the first attempt. The variability of character and the expression of the traits particular to this sign depend also largely on any additional astrological signs and their individual natal charts' positions. When trying to understand what makes your Virgo tick, you must consider any energies and nuances on his chart that can either disrupt or enhance his Virgo energies.

Quick Facts About Virgos

- They like things in a particular way.
- They are extremely logical.
- They know what they want.
- They are a total planner.
- They can solve almost any problem.
- They might seem judgmental, but they're just trying to help.
- They value loyalty.
- They can be perfectionists.
- They can be hard-headed sometimes.
- They are independent.

Obstacles that Arise When Dating a Virgo

- They might be a little too quiet.

- They might worry a lot, but usually for a good reason.

- They might criticize you a lot, but not with mean-spirited intent.

- They are even harder on themselves than on anyone else.

- They have a tendency to obsess over things.

Quick Guide to Dating A Virgo

- Choose honesty every time.

- You should care about your appearance and your smell.

- Don't be a drama queen.

- Don't keep your opinions to yourself either.

- Find their heart through their stomach.

- Be orderly.

- Trust them to lead.

Attracting the Virgo Man

If you are interested in seducing the Virgo man, you must begin with respect for his order and cleanliness. Usually, he would be slow to enter romance because he takes his time to get to know people. But, when he does know you, you must maintain a certain amount of consistency, or it will be over before it starts. This doesn't mean there will be no space for personal growth with a Virgo. All I'm saying is that you cannot pretend long with this sign.

The Virgo man puts up a cool exterior, but don't be fooled; his sensual and emotional needs run deep. You must be patient with his habit of over-analysis to reach his warm depths. Hard work and dedication must win any sign over, but even more so for the Virgo man.

Do you want to sweep him off his feet? Inspire him. He likes to be reminded of his own talents. In the search for a partner, honesty, patience, and order are prioritized. Have these, and you're already on the right track to winning his heart.

Attracting the Virgo Woman

A Virgo is typically a combination of close attention to detail, commitment, common sense, and intelligence. A female Virgo is nothing less, being unsurprisingly smart, capable, and modest.

Like the Virgo male, she values cleanliness. So, you'd better not just look good; you must be neat as well — at least within reason. She gets that not everyone is as orderly as she is, but you must make an effort. Also, your smell matters. A lot. That doesn't mean you should drown yourself in a vat of Axe, though.

Any attempts to woo this woman might seem daunting initially because she will probably wear a mask of indifference. The truth is, she is far from cold and impractical. She simply likes to be cautious and realistic about her new relationships. There is no way this woman will give herself to you without a complete scan of your personality, its pros, and cons. She feels deeply and loves unconditionally.

She is not to be pegged as materialistic or spoiled under any circumstances. She is an Earth sign so expect her to appreciate the luxuries of the world, like travel, art, the fine things of life. You're not obligated to get her these things, as she's always going to seek them out and make them happen for herself, with or without you. She also enjoys practical, thoughtful gifts.

Chapter Five: The Social Virgo

Are you that friend who always seems to have every situation all figured out? Are you discerning yet sociable? Hardworking but modest? Never arrogant but well-informed? You are a Virgo to your core, and everyone needs at least one Virgo friend.

Why The Virgo is An Amazing Friend

You are extremely organized. You have the title for the most practical and methodical sign in the zodiac. It doesn't matter if you're organizing a cocktail party or planning for a presentation at work; you are always relied on to deliver your A-game and make sure the activity goes as smoothly as silk.

I bet if your friend were to look through your phone, they'd probably find a variety of apps that help you maintain the order of things in your life. You love lists, filing systems, office stationery, and helpful apps.

You are the one friend who is as punctual as life allows. You always remember important birthdays and the solution to virtually every life problem, which always comes in handy. Your capacity to stay calm under pressure is unprecedented. Then there's that thing you do when you whip out a contingency plan when it is most needed and unexpected.

You are a knowledgeable and great conversationalist. You enjoy a stimulating conversation, a good book, and a healthy banter. You aren't the type to lean back and say, "I don't know," unless you do not know, which makes you genuinely eager to know. You're not a know-it-all; you simply like to KNOW.

You are also concerned about the thoughts and feelings of those around you, so even if you're not very vocal about it, you do your best to remain polite and inclusive.

You enjoy acquiring knowledge. But most people get surprised and unsure when you ask your thousand questions about something you don't know. You don't like this, but you get it.

Your aversion to adventure contradicts your constant thirst for knowledge, but your desire for routine and order justifies it. You may not want to go on that hike in those devilish mountains, but that doesn't stop you from encouraging a friend who actually wants to go.

Your memory is epic. You have mastered the art of recalling the little details. People catch themselves, saying, "How in the world did you recall that? We had that conversation ages ago!" Your memory is a blessing and a curse.

You always carry yourself with an air of dignity and class. Have you seen Divergent, the movie? The Erudite sector pretty much sums up the Virgo personality. There are few signs as self-respecting as your sun sign. You pride yourself on your ability to stay calm during a storm, stay away from meaningless arguments, and consider all your options before taking a stand instead of cutting corners. You have impeccable manners and always seem dressed for the occasion.

At first sight, it is easy to assume that you are incapable of letting your hair down and having fun, especially if you're caught working. Unfortunately for first impressions, they don't always matter because you can get your groove on around people you are comfortable with. Initially being reserved never hurt anyone.

You don't like to feel embarrassment because it is one of the feelings that seems to linger with you for quite a time. I know you remember all the embarrassing stuff that has made you cringe a little too often, and you've resolved never to let that happen again.

You are very perceptive and highly ambitious in every aspect of your life.

Everyone knows that your standards are higher than Ru Paul's heels, so they feel flattered when admitted into your inner circle. You like mature, intelligent, and high-achieving friends, not because you are a snob, but because you always want to get better, and you understand the influence of friends on the matter.

You rarely stay friends with people who have no sense of direction, but you stay to motivate and inspire the few times you do. If you have friends at work, trust they know how ambitious and uncompromising you are.

Despite your ambitious streak, you avoid atrocious power grabs. You prefer the long game, putting your career plan together, sticking to the schedule, and challenging the challenges. You are patient and diplomatic, which is why your schemes yield results most of the time. You don't mind the long wait.

You are always open to working on your friendships. You are a firm believer in the power of hard work. If you commit to an idea or project, you are prepared to see it through to the end. Some people might even find you a little single-minded and intense when you are zeroed in on a cause or problem. This is a handy trait for friendships.

You take no aspect of your friendship for granted, knowing that all relationships are still under development. If there is an argument, you are less likely to brush it under the rug. You'd rather tackle any problems immediately, further strengthening the friendship. You may not have a bunch of friends, but you prioritize those you do. You make one of the best friends anyone could have. Your practicality, knowledge, order, and encouragement of others are among the prized traits in healthy friendships.

You may be drawn to people with similar interests and intellect, but now and then, get with that one friend or group of friends who pull you out of your shell and throw you over the edge of a yacht. Basically, friends that make you try new things.

Virgo Friendship Compatibility with Other Signs

1. **The Virgin and the Ram:** You and Aries in a friendship? How did that even happen? Aries probably started it, being obsessed with challenges and all. You are generally a reserved person, but Aries likely interpreted that to be a sign of discernment. Winning your acceptance adds another colorful feather to their cap — and there's a lot of space on that cap. True, you are very picky with people you let into your life, but you approved of Aries because of their warmth and enthusiasm. They are generous with hugs, kisses, and encouragement. Aries admires your dedication and hard work. You don't like their "Me first" way of life, and they don't like your picky attitude.

2. **The Virgin and the Bull:** You and Taurus are naturally drawn to each other. You find great comfort in the Bull's loving and loyal nature while they appreciate your readiness to help or pitch in when they need you to. Maybe you think that Taurus can be a little complacent, and they think that you can be delusional, but if you stopped dragging the bull to territories that they'd rather not visit, maybe your friend wouldn't sigh so often. You are likely to share similar interests.

3. **The Virgin and the Twins:** You are ruled by Mercury, which is the planet for sharp intellects. Unfortunately, that's

about the extent of your similarities. While you are grounded and serious, Gemini has their head in the clouds. You are more comfortable working with concrete, logical concepts, while Gemini would rather deal with ambiguous ones. You are very cautious and secretive, while your friend would rather bare it all. Ironically, you are attracted to your differences. You also appreciate Gemini's cleverness while they appreciate your ability to fix issues.

4. **The Virgin and the Crab:** You can birth a relationship that can last for decades. As you both prefer the warmth of home, you'd rather have a quiet, cozy night by the fire than be out at the local bar, even with friends. You love Cancer for their ability to calm your burned out nerves while they love your attention to detail, how you always remember birthdays, or their best color. Your friend has the habit of hoarding, which pisses you off to no end because you thrive in order and simplicity. Your friend isn't too happy either about your frequent refusal to indulge their flights of fancy. But besides these, you two are great friends!

5. **The Virgin and the Lion:** You need a lot of courage to befriend domineering Leo. It is understandable, but considering the love and warmth oozing out of the lion. Still, it can get very exhausting, massaging Leo's ego, especially for a person as modest as you are. Leo also tires of your constant worry of impending doom. If you can focus on their many wonderful qualities like capability, intelligence, and loyalty, you can give them space and opportunity to appreciate your reliability and efficiency. You both are animal lovers, so that's a great conversation starter!

6. **The Virgin and the Virgin:** It must be lovely having a fellow Virgo as a friend. At least, you won't be worried about them placing a wet glass down on the antique table you purchased last fall or walking all over your recently polished

floor with muddy shoes. Also, the Virgo is a beautiful conversationalist so you can depend on this friend to bring you all the juicy gossip and give you a full summary of the week's best-seller without dropping spoilers. The major downside to this is that you two have a habit of feeding each other's insecurities instead of offering encouragement. You both are filled with talent and need to be open to riskier opportunities than you allow yourselves experience. You both enjoy the natural scenery, so consider long bike rides or a walk in the park.

7. **The Virgin and the Scales**: You find Libra's intelligence so satisfying. But certain things about your pal are a little hard for you to understand. For instance, Libra's avoidance of any discomfort. You prefer to deal with problems head-on before they become too much to handle. You also struggle with your friend's inability to concentrate on one subject or person for long. They also have a few issues with you. They don't appreciate advice they didn't ask for. They also don't like to manage money and be scolded for their impulsive spending.

8. **The Virgin and the Scorpion:** The mystery of the scorpion makes them a hard nut to crack, but if anyone can do it, it's you. Scorpio has an affinity for you, probably because you are always willing to assist others. You value authenticity in yourself and others. If you made a promise to help at an event, you'd be at the location thirty minutes early with anything you feel will be needed. This dedication grants you a soft spot with Scorpio. Despite the time it takes for you to build a friendship, you soon learn of the scorpion's many wonderful qualities like sensitivity, loyalty, and persistence.

9. **The Virgin and the Archer:** Sagittarius, while being full of spontaneity, is an exhausting friend for you. You both share a deep love for knowledge; but you can't seem to understand why they just won't settle down. Sagittarius, on the other hand,

is fascinated by your desire to over-analyze everything, from the cashier's hairstyle to the cat's preference for dry food. If you find a way to handle each other's mannerisms, a lot of strength can be drawn from this friendship. Allow the archer to push the boundaries of your experiences. Travel together or try out exotic cuisine. In return, your advice to get organized and become more efficient will be appreciated by the archer.

10. **The Virgin and the Sea-Goat:** It is never a surprise to see you two become fast friends. Being Earth signs, you and Capricorn have shared values. You both don't shy away from hard work and feel the happiest when doing something productive. You two also have a deep respect for family traditions and routines. There is no sign more excited about the holidays than you two. The preparations start weeks in advance, and while Capricorn can get a little domineering, you two are quick to sort out your issues and move past. They don't like it when you are overly critical of their faults, but the similarities between you two are enough to overlook any unpleasantness. The pros outweigh the cons here.

11. **The Virgin and the Water Bearer:** Nobody brings chaos to your life as much as Aquarius does, so why are you so attracted to this unconventional friend? I'll tell you why. Deep down, you are yearning for excitement. You are at your best with regularity and order, and you derive pleasure from organizing chaotic environments. But, when you feel a little bored, that's when Aquarius storms the show, proposing a nude sprint later at midnight or skinny midnight dipping in a nearby lake. Will your wild friend ever convince you to switch sides? Very unlikely, but you live vicariously through them, enjoying the show from a distance. Aquarius is one of the smartest signs of the zodiac, so I'm sure you two will get along swimmingly and may even share a love for sci-fi.

12. **The Virgin and the Fish:** Despite you two being polar opposites, the two of you become fast friends. Chaotic Pisces is grateful for the order you provide, while you enjoy their short stories. Sure, you hate it when the fish shows up an hour late to the restaurant, but you do know that your endless worrying can make you difficult. When the fish tests your patience, because they will, comfort yourself with the fact that you will never find someone who listens as perfectly. Similarly, the fish appreciates your ability to turn dreams into reality.

The Virgo at a Party

To you, people exaggerate parties. Parties are great, but overrated. People think that attendance somehow reflects their value as a person. Especially birthdays. People make a huge production out of the event, throwing all kinds of emotional tantrums if anyone as much as disregards it.

Birthdays are a huge deal, parties too. But Virgos are very low key about social events. They aren't as hung up on parties as other zodiac signs. This does not mean that they never attend parties. Sometimes, they willingly enjoy the baby shower of a loved one, a wedding party of a friend, and so on, or unwillingly enjoy a rave at the club or a frat house party.

You are usually in tune with your inner world and what you want out of life. This results in you being more concerned with what truly exists than extrinsic experiences. You are more likely to concentrate on the core symbolism of the person's birthday other than the outward displays and extras. To put it more simply, you would prefer to focus on what is in a gift box than fuss about how beautifully it was packaged. This is the reason you don't go crazy about your own birthday; you prefer to enjoy the day with people who are special to you.

"Stop trying to take me to random parties!" This is one thing you wish your friends understood. To impress a Virgo, this is not really how to go, and you may transmit the wrong message to them.

If you intend to throw a party or are to organize an event, then ironically, the Virgo is perfect at planning. They'll give you nothing less than perfection at the end. This doesn't mean they want to get down on the floor — you might need to hand them a drink or two for that.

How Virgos Make Friends

When you feel comfortable enough in an environment, you are an excellent communicator. It isn't uncommon for you to be reserved among strangers at the start, but when you've established a baseline for everyone and the environment, you're perfectly comfortable matching everyone else. In other words, you like to read the room and read people, so you know the best way to connect with them.

If You Have a Virgo Friend, Pay Attention to This.

Virgos may get the "forgive and forget" memo, but they will take out their favorite red gel pen and cross out the forget part into oblivion — especially if you continue to hurt them again and again.

Your Virgo friend will give you a shoulder to cry on when you need it, but be prepared to get a lot more than that. They will help you get back on your feet by doing all they can to remind you of why you're awesome and capable — even if it means they must physically, literally drag you out of your funk.

If you notice your Virgo friend is intensely focused on something, for the love of everything holy, that is the exact time to *not* bother them about something trivial like your hunger for Lebanese shawarma. They'll snap out of whatever they're working on if you really need their attention for something, but please make it something important.

The Virgo needs order. If you're messy, it's not going to work for them. Even if you have a room in their home to yourself, if you're messy, it's not enough for your Virgo that they *cannot see* the mess; they *know* it's there. And eventually, they will make you clean up, so you don't wind up bringing roaches, or a bad smell, or whatever it is they'd hate to their home. They also know where they put what and hate when you move it. Even when the Virgo makes a "mess," leave it as it is. There is an order that only the Virgo understands in that chaos.

If your Virgo friend spends the day lounging and doing nothing, very few miracles can draw them out. Let them have it. No one works as hard as they do.

Loyalty is everything to the Virgo. Their huge hearts that radiate so much warmth despite their ability to heavily strike anyone who tries to hurt you is only one among many reasons they are loved by all who know and understand them.

Chapter Six: Shades of Virgo

Decanate and *cusps* are astrological terms that split your sun sign into different categories. These categories further emphasize and define certain traits and qualities particular to your sun sign.

Every birth date falls within a specific decanate of a sun sign while only certain birth dates are within a cusp. Basically, every cusp is a decanate, but not all decanates are cusps.

Everyone is born within a particular decanate of a sign, and people may also be born on the cusp. In this chapter, I hope to clarify the meaning of decanates and cusps in your life.

Decans or Decanates

Each astrological sign is divided into three categories. Each is called a decan or decanate. This term originates from a Greek word *dekanoi*, which means "separated by ten days." This term was taken from the Egyptians, who had a calendar that divided each year into 360 days. The Egyptian annual calendar had twelve months per year, each containing thirty days. Every month is further split into three sections, each containing ten days. These ten-day subdivisions were called dekanoi.

Astrology still splits each zodiac into decans. Imagine the entire zodiac to be a circle. A circle measures 360 degrees, and one decan is only a 10-degree part of that circle, each one ten days long. The sun passes through the zodiac circle (all the signs), at roughly the rate of one degree a day. Note that this isn't accurate because not every month is exactly 30 days, but the math is the same.

Now, the decan of a zodiac sign doesn't alter the fundamental characteristics of the sign. Instead, it only refines and personalizes the zodiac's general traits. For instance, imagine you were born into the third decan of Aries. You are still very much an Aries; but you have now been distinguished from the Aries in the first and second decans. You are special and different from them while they are special and different from you.

Each decan is represented by a constellation in the sky. The constellations' special spiritual translation also contributes to the uniqueness and quality of individuals born under different decans.

Finally, each decan is ruled by a planet, also known as a sub ruler, because it doesn't dethrone the sign's overall ruling planet. This sub ruler, kind of like a Vice President, only works to add to or enhance the special qualities of that particular decanate.

Decans of Virgo

- Decan: First

- Date: 22nd August - 1st September

- Keyword: Analyze

- Constellation: The goblet, crater, or cup of Apollo. It represents emotional generosity.

- Sub-ruling planet: Mercury

Mercury is the planet of mental activity. It is both sub-ruler and ruler for this decan, granting you an intellect to be reckoned with. You tackle problems with rationality, always seeking the reason for everything, and then applying that knowledge to the search for a solution. More than a few times, your insightful contributions have been considered as prophetic, when they are simply results of acute observation.

You radiate a great amount of warmth and wit that attracts admirers and acquaintances. But not everyone gets a ticket into the inner chambers because you expect nothing less than decorum and intelligence in the people you call friends.

When you fall in love, you morph into a devoted, hopeless romantic who is extremely sensitive to their lover. Your calm exterior does well to hide nervous energy brewing beneath. You are prone to secretly worrying and fussing over little problems.

- Decanate: Second
- Date: 2nd September - 12th September
- Keyword: Efficient
- Constellation: Hercules, the powerful demigod who wins a victory over evil
- Sub-ruling planet: Saturn

Saturn is the planet of tenacity. This, combined with your ruling planet, gives a special edge to your personality. You are focused on the details and prefer to plan in advance to avoid mistakes.

You are usually perceived as focused and persistent when, in truth, you are mutable and versatile. Your goal is the constant demand for perfection in yourself and the determination to always outdo yourself. You are the kind of perfectionist that suffers unnecessarily when you fall short of your own expectations.

In love, you are the most sympathetic and gentle soul. You are willing to cross oceans to please your partner, who is a fast disappearing quality today. You are relatively easy to live with as long as nobody awakens your stubborn nature.

- Decanate: Third

- Date: 13th September - 22nd September

- Keyword: Discriminate

- Constellation: The bear driver or the old herdsman. The symbol of using wisdom

- Sub-ruling planet: Venus

Venus is the planet of pleasure. The outgoing and welcoming qualities of this sub-ruler combined with Mercury signifies that you have a way of winning people over. Approval is your major motivator. You are a connoisseur of expression, using written and spoken words. You are simply charming with an air of creativity and perfect use of color represented in your appearance or surroundings.

Your sense of style is always properly interpreted, and this projects a powerful personal image of who you are. Confidence and carriage are your major assets in the work environment, and you are recognized for your diplomacy and sensitivity.

You find no joy living under limitations, so you are attracted to creative adventures where you have free creative control. When you fall in love, you are generous and warm, despite your almost incessant demand for attention.

Cusps

Have you ever, at any point, felt like you were a mixture of two zodiac signs? Like you may be a Pisces, but also something else? It's like having one leg in two nearby countries, and it is called a cusp. Every zodiac sign has its cusps, a combination of two zodiac signs. It is common to find people who are Scorpios but have Sagittarius qualities. Many people were born at the end or the start of a zodiac sign, which can lead to confusion when trying to determine their place in astrology.

When a person's birth date falls within a few days of the sun's transition from one sign to the next, it means that the person was born on a cusp and their personality can be affected by the two distinct zodiac signs.

A cusp is an invisible barrier that separates a pair of zodiac signs next to each other. With this sun's disc being roughly half a degree wide, it is possible for the sun to create a cusp as it moves through all the signs. This movement causes the solar disc to be halfway into the next zodiac, with the rest remaining in the present one.

Place a red cup and a blue cup side by side on the ground, with an inch between them. Draw a line in the middle and slowly move a matchbox from one side to the other. During movement, observe the period when half of the box is on the red side while the other is on the blue side. That, my dear, is a cusp!

The Significance of a Cusp

Birthdate on a cusp makes you a hybrid of the two signs. The energies emanating from the two signs may not get along, or they might... either way, every individual born on a cusp acquires certain qualities, based on the cusp you were born into:

1. Power cusp: 16th - 22nd April

2. Energy cusp: 17th - 23rd May

3. Magic cusp: 17th - 23rd June

4. Oscillation cusp: 19th - 25th July

5. Exposure cusp: 19th - 25th August

6. Beauty cusp: 19th -25th September

7. Revolution cusp: 18th - 24th December

8. Prophecy cusp: 18th - 24th December

9. Mystery cusp: 16th - 23rd January

10. Sensitivity cusp: 15th - 21st February

Virgo Cusps

Cusp: Virgo-Leo
Date: 23rd - 27th August.

You are Virgo with a dash of Leo. Your reliability, generosity, and graciousness attract people to you like a moth to a flame. You are also known for your creative streak and a great sense of fashion. You are noticeably witty, optimistic, and fascinating. Undertaken projects almost always turn out to be a success because of your keen attention to detail and quick thinking. It isn't uncommon to see you in charge of events because your organizational skills are legendary among the zodiac signs. This can make you a little impatient with others who are not as quick-witted as you are, but that usually inspires your colleagues' responsibility and creativity. Social settings bring out your best qualities. When in love, you are unreserved, fiercely loyal, and warm.

Cusp: Virgo-Libra
Date: 18th - 22nd September

You have Virgo and a little Libra in you. You are perceptive, intelligent, and in love with ideas! You are naturally outgoing and have a way of getting through to people on a psychological level. Your mind is always buzzing with ideas or information, and that makes you always in the mood for stimulating conversations. Your social skills are most valuable in a work environment. You are a lover of beauty and aesthetics, making you prone to becoming a collector of rare and beautiful items or engaging in creative adventures.

Chapter Seven: The Professional Virgo

There's that one employee who does things the right way to a fault at every workplace; they show up a half-hour earlier than most workers and drive everyone nuts with their perfectionist and detail-oriented attitude to work. That person is most likely a Virgo.

Everyone knows how particular and neat you are, with your million to-do lists and properly organized notes. You are a good enough team player, but you prefer your own creative space to just do what you do best. You wish someone would just hand you that autonomy you desire so much.

As expected, you thrive in work environments where rules sustain the profession's untainted reputation. As much as anyone can do almost any job with proper training and dedication, certain professions are better suited to your unique talents, Virgo.

> 1. **A Writer:** Since you have a great many thoughts flowing through your mind at any point, and you love to have your own space to work, then you would excel as a writer. You love being on your own. The only other thing you might enjoy more than cracking open a good book is penning one down yourself, or at least challenging yourself to do just that.

2. **An Accountant:** I have mentioned your keen attention to detail often now because it's one of your most popular and most prized qualities because it always comes in handy. Combined with your understanding of numbers and critical attitude, you almost seem like the perfect candidate for this job. This career path allows you to satisfy your need to go over things as many times as you need to be certain. It's challenging to handle another person's money, but your discipline ensures that your moral compass stays facing the right direction. Similar careers include bookkeeper, auditor, hedge fund manager, and coder.

3. **A Nutritionist:** You want to make the world a better place, and one way to do that is to teach people better ways of taking better care of themselves through their eating habits. Add that to your existing fascination with nutrition and health, and you are all set for a satisfying profession. Everyone knows that Virgo enjoys practicing what they preach. Chances are, they already practiced it a thousand times before the preaching started. You'd rather teach from experience, am I right? Similar career paths include masseuse, life coach, and dietician.

4. **An Acupuncturist:** You already have an interest in natural healing methods and health, so this would be a satisfying path for you to tread. You enjoy testing out herbs, health hacks, vitamins, etc. Studying the science behind this practice is a common practice for members of your sun sign. Similar career paths include yoga instructor, holistic healer, reiki healer, and natural pathologist.

5. **A Professional Housekeeper:** If your daily life is a nonstop swirl of laundry, organizing, straightening, and housework, turning this natural sense of order and aesthetics into a job will fully maximize the perfectionist in you. Similar

career paths include personal assistant, home stager, wedding planner, and professional organizer.

6. **An Executive Assistant:** No one is quite as organized as you are. Combine this with your eagle focus, attention to detail, and efficiency, and you become the perfect executive assistant. These are the perfect traits to possess when organizing schedules for yourself and others, especially if the other person is a celebrity or a company's CEO. You are excellent at organizing schedules, meetings, functions, and trips, and will not make a fuss if your boss adds a few tasks like house-sitting, miscellaneous duties, and shopping. You will organize things either way, why not get a paycheck to boot?

7. **A Statistician:** Your obsession with details makes this an excellent career for you. It isn't the easiest job to do, but an opportunity to collect and analyze statistics for a company or the government will surely put your best skills on display. Similar career paths include geologist, auditor, research analyst, consultant, and forest ranger.

8. **An Archivist:** This is another career that will exalt your penchant for categorizing and sorting. This job demands attention to detail, which is not only your forte but also a part of yourself that can't be ignored. You will find this satisfying. Similar career paths include art historian, archeologist, museum director, bookkeeper, and so on.

9. **A Computer Engineer:** When there's a fault with systems workflow or information output, you are the ideal person for the job (with proper training, of course). You are infinitely patient, a necessity when dealing with faulty technology. No sign will take their time like you will, to find and erase all the duplicate files and junk information, rebuilding the system, and ensuring they run as smoothly as possible. Similar paths include electricians, town planners, and systems analysts.

10. **A Laboratory Technician:** Your unique talents make you perfectly suited for this job. Gathering data, keeping records, sorting information, and compiling reports is the perfect activity to keep you mentally engaged and give you the satisfaction you derive from orderliness. Your thoroughness, focus, and ability to create results are legendary. You might drive your colleagues nuts with the amount of time you take to work or your occasional need to take "one last look" at the material, but they know that you always deliver impeccably. Similar career paths include scientists, data analysts, biochemists, and surveyors.

11. **A Welder:** This work requires a high level of concentration, a steady hand, and accuracy. One wrong move and the project could develop uneven edges or cracks. Even worse, the whole structure could collapse, but not on your watch. You make sure that every weld is performed with utmost accuracy to the standard of the industry. Similar career paths include craftsman, architect, sculptor, furniture designer, and ceramicist.

The Virgo as an Employee

You are an idealist to your core. Your idealism is an asset in the workplace, and people know it. When given a task, you throw yourself into its center and remain submerged until it is done. While Aries and Capricorn are like you in this way, what separates you from the bunch is your determination to do the job to the highest quality in your rulebook. You do this not because you like to be better than others, but because you believe that a thing worth doing should be done well.

You don't appreciate inferior performances or a job that wasn't done whole heartedly, which is why everyone you work with knows that any project you embark on will be completed with utmost precision and care. A Virgo is an excellent worker.

You function meticulously. This is another trait that closely follows the unyielding need for perfection. When given a task, you dive into the heart of the issue and analyze it, leaving no stones unturned. If there is a high-profile assignment or project that requires utmost attention and thoroughness, they most likely have your number on speed dial. You are not like Gemini, whose attention is fleeting, taking them from one incomplete task to another. Or Aquarius, who is a master at envisioning abstract ideas. You can't help but lavish attention on the job at hand, considering every clarification and clause. This alone is enough reason for you to excel in fields like fashion, banking, law, and others that demand an acute eye for detail and an unwavering concentration.

You are not afraid to dish out criticism. As a Virgo employee, you will gladly point out any flaws in the system — even if you're the reason the flaws exist. You're not afraid to own your mistakes. If the boss caused the problem, that doesn't exempt them from your criticism either, especially when you deem it necessary. This is because you exalt perfection over the sacredness of titles and positions.

If you're an intern or a fresh recruit, keep your criticisms in check for the time being, until you get the lay of the land and understand the power dynamics at play. Usually, this should take you about three months. Don't just jump in with your stick, poking bears willy-nilly.

That said, it would be a lot easier if your coworkers can try to remember that as a Virgo, your overly critical behavior doesn't come from a place of hatred or malice, but a desire to see everyone do better. You're not in the habit of tolerating work that is less than standard, and you are willing to do whatever it takes to get quality.

You are grounded. (No, not that kind of ground.) As a Virgo, your primary element is Earth, and this is consistent with your grounded, practical, down-to-earth personality. You are practical and only concern yourself with activities that seem to have a promising outcome. You are blessed with a discriminating eye and sensible mind, which draws you only to pursuits that can reach a logical end.

You are not like dreamy Pisces whose imagination seems to flow in whatever direction they please or like Gemini, who has an airy brilliance about them. So, you are the ideal choice for positions that entail an incessant focus and strong analytical skills.

Another professional field where your intrinsic skills come in handy is the service sector like charity, health, banking and finance, entertainment (think writing, directing, continuity, and so on), education, hospitality, and much more. These and similar fields put you in your element because of your constant readiness to help others, another key trait of your Sun sign.

You are all too willing to bury yourself underneath a ton of commitment and hard work if you know that you are making life better for someone somewhere. This is probably because of your ruling planet Mercury, who was depicted in ancient Roman mythology as an impossibly busy god, who was always found in a race against time to deliver messages to and from divine entities.

You may become a workaholic if you aren't one already. The major disadvantage of your highly industrious and meticulous persona is that you are prone to becoming a workaholic. You display symptoms of the no *play- just work* syndrome. Five in every seven Virgos are workaholics, and you may just be in the majority. You are a firm believer in service first and leisure later.

Everyone you work with appreciates your workaholic nature, even you, considering it skyrockets you up the professional ladder. But it also comes with an added unhealthy lifestyle. Think of a buy-one-get-one-free situation. When a person, no matter the zodiac, is cooped up inside almost every time, focused on work with so much nervous intensity, they become prone to a variety of health concerns.

However, if you have Virgo employees, give them a break when they feel under the weather because it's rare, actualized Virgo who will take one themselves. If you are a Virgo employee, make the most of your weekend — and not by working incessantly. Don't worry about a dive in your productivity because there's no doubt about your ability to get the job done. I mean, it is you, after all.

Your zodiac has a significant impact on your personality, which makes you, a Virgo, an asset to your field. This isn't simply because of your meticulous and dedicated attitude to work and everything. It is also because you are one of the few employees that thrive with or without supervision.

Granted, sometimes you work really slowly because of the amount of caution you exert when performing a task. But you can be trusted to work alone because your mind runs a lot of miles per minute, and you have a strong sense of responsibility and work ethic.

The Virgo Boss

As a boss, you enjoy blending into the background while remaining present and keeping your eye on your workplace. You like to stay involved in everything happening around you while still giving your employees enough space to do their work.

Being in a position of power doesn't affect your willingness to get your hands dirty when necessary. You like having a personal but professional relationship with the people that work for you. As mentioned earlier, you like to be present and in touch with the work environment, employees included.

You request team meetings, reports on everything and anything being done right now and soon. You like to know because you are not fond of unwelcome surprises, especially at work. Everything must be organized from start to finish.

You also want to be in touch with those who work for you. You'll have team meetings, want reports on everything being done, what's happening next, and the whole plan of execution from start to finish.

At your best, you can be a kindhearted, soft, and trusted adviser who is excellent at analysis and decision making. You give specific instructions on how to do what needs to be done and sometimes lend a hand when you think is necessary.

At your worst: You become a fussy micromanager who judges and criticizes without sympathy. You not only watch everyone like a hawk, but you also waste no time pointing out every flaw and every wrong move. You become insatiable. So, what's the fix?

The Introverted Style of Leadership

This kind of leadership is ideal in any productive work environment. Here, you should exhibit a quietness and tenderness that commands respect while still leaving you approachable. Listen more than you speak and render advice more than you complain, instead of commanding everyone's attention and interrupting discussions.

This style of leadership will leave you flexible and receptive to daring projects and new ideas. This will encourage constructive criticism and suggestions from your employees, which you should carefully pay attention to, leaving your mind open to new information. This creates a better work environment with employees who feel heard and valued, which increases motivation, proactivity, and productivity.

If Your Boss is Virgo...

The most vital thing to remember when working for a Virgo boss is this: know exactly what you're trying to say! This means having all your figures, details, and facts on hand when interacting with them. They think through every single word you speak, so say what you mean. It is relatively easy to work under a Virgo boss. All you need to do is:

1. Be proactive and be hardworking.

2. Obey all company policies and follow necessary procedures.

3. Know your job and avoid making mistakes.

4. Prepare to support your suggestions with logic and feasible evidence.

5. Make sure that you and your work area are neat and tidy.

6. Dress modestly and neatly.

7. Keep emotions and sentiments off the work unless sentiment is required to do your job, like with service providers.

8. This might seem irrelevant but don't gossip, especially behind your boss' back.

9. Take responsibility for your mistakes and immediately act to correct any damage you've done.

Once you have made the necessary adjustments to your boss' calm, professional, and perfectionist attitude, you will see her best qualities bursting through the seams. Let's run through these qualities.

Tender, just, and helpful: Your Virgo boss may drop many criticizing remarks about the project you are working on, but she will also show you a way out of your dilemma and request the corrections repeatedly to be sure that you are on the right track. She will make sure that everything you need to do a stellar job is provided to leave no room for excuses. She may even offer her help sometimes. Her kindness is not limited to professional issues. If you need a break or an off day for important personal matters or an illness, she will understand.

Trustworthy: Trust is a huge deal for the Virgo boss. But you will uncover just how unbiased, kind and helpful he is when you have his trust. Don't forget that the Virgo is more sensitive than he seems on the outside, and would like to be assured that her help isn't taken for granted. Most bosses are grateful for a thank you note, but the Virgo boss will be really impressed by one. He will feel more appreciative and touched by your gratitude than most.

Zero small talks: Have you noticed that your Virgo boss isn't into any kind of small talk? She is not the type to engage in conversations at the workplace unrelated to work unless you two have a personal relationship outside of work. If not, expect no kind of chit chat. She maintains openness and clarity when communicating about work-related issues and is a pro at giving positive feedback if it is deserved. She has no problems making her employees feel appreciated and seen. Negative thoughts she might want to share about your work will usually be done in private, to preserve your dignity and reputation in the work environment.

Calm and lenient: despite his desire for perfection and his discerning eye, he is a relaxed and open-minded person to work for. These attributes make the work environment less tense, comfortable, and more productive. Think of him as a boss who might seem bossy but really isn't. He is modest in professional behavior, interpersonal relationships, and appearance.

Obstacles the Virgo Faces at Work

Your keen sense of observation: While one of your prized traits in the work environment, it is also the culprit behind your anxiety. You tend to look back to a problem you experienced so many years ago and cringe at the thought. You couldn't believe it happened, and you blame yourself. This leads to self-doubt and excessive, unnecessary worrying.

Life struggles are real, and it isn't easy for you to be overwhelmed with so much natural optimism, but you can counteract this by consciously deciding to always see the good in situations and people. Focus on the times when you were simply badass. You did it before, so you can do it again. Be grateful for all that you are and have.

Your tendency to critique others: You are great at critical thinking, but you are also popular for how much criticism you give to others. It is understandable to want to help others, but you need to remember that not everyone appreciates unsolicited opinions.

You also need to water down your criticisms before sharing them, because some people are more sensitive than others, and you don't want to go around hurting people's feelings, do you? The end doesn't always justify the means, remember that.

Your stubbornness: When you imagine an idea or a thing you want, you whip out your imaginary ear lids and call it a day. You can sometimes be averse to opinions, even the good ones. You can be defiant, but don't have to be. It is okay to have preferences and want things to go a certain way.

But leave room for suggestions and growth. Unexpected situations and factors can be helpful. You may not believe this, but everything happens for a reason, and it is absolutely impossible to control everything. Leave room for flexibility.

Your tendency to worry too much: You enjoy knowing that everyone around you is happy, and even more so if you are the reason for this happiness. This can mean pushing yourself to extremely uncomfortable lengths to please people, especially at work. You need to remember to choose yourself sometimes. Your needs, health, and happiness matter too. If you need to call in sick, do it. If you cannot take on a project for personal reasons, that's okay too.

Your tendency to get frustrated easily: As a perfectionist, you can be your own worst critic. You do not allow yourself to be anything less than the perfect image of yourself in your head. You will literally ruin an entire project because you don't think you did it perfectly. First, breathe. Nobody is perfect. It is okay to make mistakes. It is okay to do your best and leave the rest.

Your penchant for overthinking: You just love to overthink everything, don't you? This can be a good thing and a bad thing. Go over facts, ideas, and situations thoroughly before deciding. But overthinking can also make you see things that aren't there. Again, breathe. Trust your gut, forgive yourself for past mistakes, and let things go.

Your unwavering demand for independence: You like to do this by yourself, and that is admirable. I am a firm believer of "if you want something done right, do it yourself." But it is okay to ask for help when you need it. You may not be comfortable bothering people, but there are those who will readily help you because they love you or they are being paid to. Either way, take it!

Your inclination to be choosy: You are precise, and that is a quality that makes you excel among your peers. But make space in your life for new and different experiences. You never know where they'll take you or what you will learn.

Chapter Eight: Virgo Sexual Compatibility

Knowing all your sun sign qualities, you know that you make an attentive and patient lover. This can be infuriating for people looking for a quick rump. You prefer to concentrate on your lover's preferences, possessing almost biological knowledge of their erogenous zones. This makes you one of the most sensual and desirable lovers of the zodiac.

But you tend to give yourself too much of yourself to others to the detriment of your own sexual needs. You need to allow yourself to be pleasured as intensely as you do others. Remember, sex need not be perfect or neat. It is more enjoyable when mutual and packed with spontaneity. We all know you're great in bed, but let's see how great in bed you are with other signs.

Virgo and Aries

This is definitely a hot match. Aries is more than capable of sweeping you off your feet before you even blink. This is very exciting if you are in the market for fast, furious, and nasty. But you are likely to catch yourself stopping everything in its tracks by saying something like, "You won't even take me to dinner at least?" Everyone on the block knows that Aries doesn't like to beat about the bush, especially with sex. But you kind of like information about who you're swapping body juices with.

In the bedroom, kitchen, or car, Aries is effortlessly passionate and sexy, but not the most considerate. This might irk you unless you somehow decide to make it your goal to fix it. You could enjoy yourself while allowing Aries to fall right into your plans to become an all-knowing parent. You don't even have to bother about looking for complex ways to seduce this person because many Aries people go about their day in an almost perpetual state of arousal.

Surprisingly, a lot of Aries folk know their need for the guidance and help you will gladly provide. In gratitude to you for the tips on sex positions and simple table etiquette, Aries will bathe you in adoration. They are the kind to barge into your office to inform you that you will be carted off to a fancy adventure sure to end with two of you tangled up in the sheets.

Aries is strong and highly active, with almost no tolerance for many things. So, if you are searching for a person who will drag you out of your hole, be responsive to and be grateful for your grounding influences, Aries is the one for you! This will finally teach you to allow yourself to go and be sexy.

Virgo and Taurus

This reasonable and logical person will tickle your senses from day one. The many similarities between you two will guarantee a quick friendship. Taurus will be capable of acquiring all the material possessions you consider being of value, but cannot survive with anything less than the highest amount of luxury. You might also find aspects of this sign's preferences baffling, like why a person believes in the necessity of a solid gold key holder.

But, when sex is brought to the table, you might see the light in Taurus' desire to just lay in luxury. Taurus's planetary ruler is Venus, the planet of desire, and this usually brings a sensual touch to this Earthy sign. Instead of your reaction to things you feel and see in terms of what you can gain or learn from it, Taurus usually just does it because it feels good. Snap! Like that.

This means you must let go of a lot of thoughts while sex is happening, and just connect with your instincts. Taurus will pretty much respond to anything you do, so don't overthink it. Over time, you both will get along more easily than you did at first, but certain adjustments might need to be made to keep the sexual fire burning. This will reduce your overthinking a little and simply allow yourself to indulge yourself now and then.

Virgo and Gemini

You and that chatterbox sign are naturally drawn to each other. This is because you both share the same planetary ruler, Mercury. Gemini manifests the daytime energy of Mercury, smoky mirrors and tricks, while you are the planet's nighttime side. You think through everything that you feel through your senses and try to categorize them. You have developed a method of seeing the order in everything.

Chaotic Gemini will like this about you and will need your help. You might notice this before sex, but everything becomes crystal clear when you do. While you're setting the mood, Gemini talks the entire time, so you might have to think of ways to relax them.

When the verbal part of your time with each other ends, you are likely to experience a very satisfying connection with Gemini. Your vast knowledge of human anatomy and its pleasures will astound them because they probably didn't know about this much sexual information! They will also do everything in their power to please you. But you must remember to be vocal and clear when telling Gemini what you like. This experience will teach you there is always something new to learn from everyone, despite how people look. Gemini's many notes and observations will fascinate you for quite a time.

Virgo and Cancer

This moody, messy and sensitive sign will draw you in because it feels like you have found a true companion. You both are very concerned about caring for others and rendering services to people who need them. The difference between your acts of service is that Cancer would rather get in there and do things for people, while you take more of a life coach approach. This manifests most beautifully in bed.

You will instinctively know the Cancer's needs because you just have a weird way of knowing what will benefit people. You two might experience the wrong kind of friction if you get trapped in a loop of unwillingness to be pleased. Cancer is quick to figure out what you want and will go to great lengths to please you. They also expect you to appreciate the good loving you're getting.

You will also need to take great care in handling Cancer's fragile feelings. They might not appreciate your subtle suggestions and hints. Eventually, there could be a possibility you both become exhausted from trying to outdo each other sexually. This is a great match if you're looking for a quick affair. The lesson to learn here should be obvious now. Forget everything you have internalized about receiving sexual pleasure. It can be just as fun as giving.

Virgo and Leo

This sign is flashy, very sexy, and dashing. They will capture your attention without even breaking a sweat. You might notice a few flaws here and there, like a tiny, creased part of their shirt, but quickly, you'll be accepting of this fabulously wrapped package that oozes undeniable style.

Don't even think of suggesting the sexual activity because this spirited sign would rather be the one to get the ball rolling. Once the majestic lion is finally finished sweeping you off your feet, you'll see that their roar is not even as scary as a nibble. The lion is a huge stuffed bear that gets cozy in your arms and takes all the love that can be given.

Despite Leo's tendency to be domineering and demanding in daily life, this sign is one of the most generous signs of the zodiac. They are generous souls that get a kick from pleasing you. That said, the Leo gets their ego stroked by the number of times they can make you lose it. Leo can be very noisy, with a voracious appetite. If you two decide to go further than a quick tangle, you may need to tame their pride a little. If you succeed, you are guaranteed a lover forever.

Virgo and Virgo

Meeting a Virgo like yourself can be quite a rewarding experience for the two of you. Not only will there be countless similarities like ideas, ethics, and tastes, but the sexual pull between you will also be approved of by both parties. Now that you have met someone as reserved as you are, it could be awhile before a move is made in the sensual direction, but that's cool. Just imagine the things that get your engine going, like the fact that there's finally someone to care for you.

When you both get tangled up, it's easy for you both to know where the major buttons are. There might be an initial struggle or competition to outdo each other, but things will be smooth sailing from there when you find your rhythm. There is a lot of potential for this to develop into a long-term relationship. Unlike the pairing between you and a few other signs, there is no competition for attention between you two. If a relationship stems from this passionate affair, you both could become too comfortable with each other.

Do your best to keep things interesting between you. Throw variety into the mix by going on short getaways occasionally; just don't spend every single second together. Here, the quote, "Absence makes the heart grow fonder," has never been more fitting. Being apart for a little time will grant you two the opportunity to see why you want to get together again. The lesson you will learn from this is to remain open to the possibility of finding someone as thoughtful, generous, and almost as perfect as you are.

Virgo and Libra

Libra's enticing exterior will pull you in, especially because of how hard it will be for you to point out a crack in their shell. The Libra is almost always as beautiful as they come. Their taste, eye for beauty, and uncanny intelligence are also something you find very impressive.

You may be completely aware of the tangible sexual tension between the two of you that is like an invisible string connecting your bodies. But it will still be a challenge getting Libra to even seem affected by your sexual advances. Libra is a hopeless romantic with high expectations of the perfect fairytale romance. These expectations can be a little unrealistic, even for you. But you enjoy a challenging experience and will jump right in.

Look forward to a little negotiation before you can finally take them to bed. Libra will be comfortable knowing you are worthy of the amount of romantic devotion they can give to their lover. Libra brings their delicate touch and old fashioned sensuality to the bedroom, which impresses you. In return, you do exactly what they want, how they want it, almost effortlessly.

But tread carefully because they tend to be all too willing to let you please every physical need without returning the favor. This will definitely work against the sustenance of a long-term relationship if you ever begin one. Put up solid boundaries and layout your expectations. Whether you're interested in much more than a one-night stand or not, you will learn a valuable lesson from this experience. Spending time around incredibly beautiful people like Libras will make you feel closer to that perfection you've always yearned for.

Virgo and Scorpio

Getting to know Scorpio can be a daunting experience for you. At first, you might feel like a deer caught in headlights or like a character in Dorothy's squad when they finally met the wizard of Oz. Scorpio will ooze the energy of a guru, resolute but quiet. They are naturally confident people, and this can make them seem very intimidating. Don't overthink it, though; your efforts to always improve their experience with you will earn you points.

The Scorpio will quickly take to the bedroom to get you thinking about sex in a whole new light. Once they have their arms around and on you, you may feel your soul literally taking breaks from your body. Scorpio is here to take you to the edges of pleasure and give you a hard shove, making your whole body ache as your first orgasm rips through you.

The Scorpio will be very impressed with your knowledge and ability to hold your own. Regardless of their reputation for being manipulative and possessive, Scorpio prefers the company of those who can stand their ground. They admire those who avoid being overwhelmed by the sheer euphoria that accompanies the experience of sex with a master. If you are thinking toward a long term relationship, you may succeed.

While you are on the receiving end of their love and loyalty, you provide suggestions and helpful hints for dealing with tiny details they are usually too busy to tend to. Here you will learn that sex is full of magic and mysticism.

Virgo and Sagittarius

This gregarious and carefree Sagittarius is very appealing, as you will see on the first date. The both of you will have no problems getting along because you are both capable of adapting to varying situations without letting a little wind throw you off course.

Sagittarius does not need that much of an incentive to walk into a lair prepared strictly for sexual stimulation. The only issue is your inability to keep them from wandering around. A Sagittarius requires enough space to exercise the beast that lives within. You can interpret this either metaphorically or literally, but it is wise to remove any delicate items or values from the scene or scenes of action.

The spirited Sagittarius causes minor but costly accidents when overly excited, especially when they get a taste of what you're capable of in bed. They are almost incapable of staying in touch with their humanity during sex, but this can be a good thing as you'll probably get your kicks from their enthusiastic reactions to your techniques.

If this experience stretches into the long term, you both might have to figure out a way around your different schedules. While you like being informed of any plans in advance, your lover is not only always geared up for the next adventure; they live in anticipation of exciting new places to visit every day. Indulge your Sagittarius sometimes. Here you'll learn that things can just float where they will, trusting that everything will return to normal when you're ready.

Virgo and Capricorn

This seemingly conservative person will pique your curiosity right away. Finally, a person you consider worthy of the type of service you enjoy providing. Meanwhile, Capricorn would rather bite their own tongue than tell you they appreciate your willingness to deal with the tiny details. You might expect a basic night of passion with this one, but you couldn't be more wrong.

Your skills and vast experience with the human body will not be a novelty to Capricorn. The sea-goat doesn't climb down the ladder of success to mingle with the rest of us for no reason. This sign, which seems like an serious workaholic, can suddenly transform into a fun and spontaneous personality. You are both Earth signs, so trust the Capricorn knows how to get freaky and dirty too.

If you are uncomfortable with any fetish or even a straightforward attack, you better watch out. Capricorn will show you different shades of horny! You'll enjoy the show, of course, as long as Capricorn is trustworthy enough to let what happened in Vegas stay in Vegas. Capricorn is also big on trust, so you can rest assured that the events of the night don't see the light of day.

It is possible to form a long-term relationship with this sign if you avoid taking on the role of constant warden. When Capricorn transforms back into the role of a cold-hearted executive, you might feel put off. The lesson you will learn from this is that it is sometimes necessary to submerge yourself in the depths of sexual sensations.

Virgo and Aquarius

Aquarius is popular for their eccentric behavior and ability to stay detached, but once you spend more time with this spirited person, you forgive a few quirks. Aquarius somehow always has a story to tell, and you enjoy good stories even though you spend more time poking holes than listening.

Really take this relationship to the physical stage immediately because the journey to similar mental levels will not be a natural one. If you must understand this water bearer, you need to recognize and respect people who not only reason outside the box but also live there.

You'll quickly realize how this comes in handy in the bedroom. Aquarius is most receptive when they are fully convinced that you agree with them on a lot of things. Their tendency to form boundaries based on political and social viewpoints is a part of what makes them such great visionaries.

Aquarius might have a hard time forgetting the exact quality of your sheets, but if you hit them in all their right places, the size of the carbon footprint you just made will not matter in the slightest. There's a slim chance that you see eye to eye with Aquarius, so it may not be possible to have a serious relationship with this sign. Whether you both hit it and quit it or you're in for the long term, you can learn a lesson from this. Acceptance is a valid precedent of love, and it should always be mutual.

Virgo and Pisces

It makes little sense that this absent-minded and seemingly incapable Pisces is the perfect match for you, but that's what it is!

You'll see why once you begin to drown in their eyes. While you have views and ideas basically set in stone, Pisces exists in an entirely different world. Actually, when you talk to the fish, you may notice that the bridge between what many people term *reality* and where the fish goes is small. This will awaken a great amount of desire to care for your fish. The Pisces will become interested once they realize that you know how to transform their lives from unbearable to exciting.

Your willingness to meet each other halfway will reveal an adventure that heals the many emotional wounds you may have. Visiting the dreamy world through experience in Pisces' bed now and then is the ideal cure for your sometimes-rigid way of life. You will be completely unaware of what hit you, but that trip to ecstasy that is sex with Pisces will be worth it. The experience is a transformative one, so it will be difficult for you to avoid having a serious relationship with this sign. The lesson to take home from this is that the perfect way to deal with all your worries is to relax and allow the Fish to love you until you completely let go.

Chapter Nine: The Moon Sign

The moon's location in your horoscope is the second most important astrological factor after the sun's location. Your sun sign influences the aspect of your personality that is most clear on the surface. It is the factor that influences how others perceive you. On the other hand, the moon sign is the aspect of your personality that exists within you. It is the factor that influences how you see *yourself.*

In the world of astrology, the moon signifies instincts, feelings, and the unconscious, while your sun sign reflects your will, your moon sign reflects your instinctive responses. The most popular astrologer of the early 20th century, Evangeline Adams, stated that a person's sun sign represented their individuality while their moon sign represented personality.

Over the years, different astrologers have defined the sun's effect to be a vital force, while the moon's effect is deemed an inherent force. In simple terms, the moon is responsible for the part of you that responds before you even take time to think.

The differences between the sun's impact and the moon in astrology are the predecessor of the theory of the *Id* and the *Ego* by Sigmund Freud. Sigmund's theory states that the ego is human consciousness, represented by the sun in astrology, and the Id is the human instinct, represented by the moon.

Your moon persona is the part you hide from everyone else. Humans have a tendency to condemn instinctive behavior, calling it primitive, brutish, and uncivilized. This is why your moon persona is that aspect of your that you consider unsettling. It is who you really are at your core, that part of you that freely entertains feelings of jealousy and hate, fear and uncertainty, even desires that you are too ashamed to admit to yourself. This is surely not the entire picture of the moon's impact on your identity.

Your moon sign is also responsible for the part of you that acts on spontaneity. It is the part of you that shows true pleasure and happiness, the part responsible for your response to emotional stimuli. The moon heavily influences the side of you that finds pleasure in the little passions of life, like the sweet scent of flowers, the smell of the Earth after a heavy rain, the joy that comes after a long soak in the tub. The moon is inseparably connected to your responses to your immediate environment. This is because the moon has dominion over the five physical senses; hearing, touch, sight, taste, and smell.

In the world of astrology, the symbolism of the moon can be complicated or even cryptic. It also represents your responses from infancy to childhood. It symbolizes your memories, your past, and your dreams. These can be said to form your inner psyche.

Landis Knight Green, a well-known astrologer, said that the moon is the beginning of the subconscious. Your moon identity is most expressed in dreams, the daydreams you ignore while you continue with your daily activities, and the sleeping dreams that plague your mind in your waking moments.

The moon's power over human emotion is the reason for its influence in your openness to others and their feelings about you. This obviously means that the moon has a major influence on romantic relationships. A solid and sustainable emotional connection is usually indicated by the woman having her moon in the same position as the man's sun. For instance, if he is a Cancer sun sign and her moon is in Cancer, they have an amazing chance of experiencing a long and happy relationship because they will both have a deep comprehension of one another.

You must have wondered, at least once, how two people born under the same sun sign can have such different personalities. This usually leads to a question, "What are their moon signs?" I'll explain this using two popular entertainers with their sun in Sagittarius. Bette Midler and Woody Allen.

The two share the same birthday and month, being 1st December, but not the same year. Allen was born in 1935, while Midler was born in 1944. The two people express powerful Sagittarian traits like frankness, humor, autonomy, and true freedom of expression.

Woody Allen is an intelligent, humorous man with barbed humor appealing to intellectuals. Being an auteur, he is a screenwriter, producer, and director who even acts in his own movies created outside the studio.

Bette Midler's career started as unconventional comedy performances in the bathhouses found in lower Manhattan. Her audiences were mostly homosexuals. But she moved on to major performances on stage and television, in movies, as a comedian and singer. She is famous for her dramatic performances, always portraying characters that are a tad too outrageous, dauntless, and wacky.

These are two entertainers who have spent years in the entertainment industry, growing and eventually breaking free of limitations to express their unorthodox ideas using their senses of humor. Let's probe deeper.

Woody Allen's moon is in Aquarius. This is responsible for his displays of rebellion. His moon sign is expressed in his free-thinking attitude of a typical Aquarius-moon personality in complete control of his life. In his private life, workplace and politics, he is progressive, unorthodox, and radical. He also portrays the emotional detachment long associated with Aquarius. His roles in films are not full of passion; his characters communicate incisively about life and its conditions, but not so it captures his audience's emotions. Rather, they intellectually stimulate in a typical Aquarius fashion and make people laugh.

People born when the moon is in Aquarius have no problem with ending a relationship (and even doing it coldly). The public has seen this in the continuous private soap operas featuring Woody Allen and the women in his life.

Bette Midler was born with her moon in Cancer, and there is a certain emotional quality that can be perceived in her. She communicates an intense amount of emotion in her work. The characters she portrays display a vulnerability usually associated with Cancer. She takes the roles of brave, lovable, and adorable women who reach out to others and care for them.

As a musical artist, Bette released hit songs that contained a deep emotional significance like The Wind Beneath My Wings, which was about a supportive partner, another Cancer value. Her personal life is very private, a major characteristic of Cancer. She is blessed with a stable and lasting union with children.

Throughout history, people have feared, worshipped, and studied the moon. From the information obtained from relics about the ancient civilizations, say that the Moon entity, usually female, always ruled beside the Sun. Certain religions even considered the Moon to be stronger than the sun because it was the seat of spiritual knowledge and wisdom.

There is a day set aside by the Romans to celebrate the Moon. This name has stood the test of time, even until today. It is now called Monday, instead of the Moon day. Scientists have been studying the power of the moon over tides, fertility, plant life, menstruation, crime, emotion, and biorhythms. Astrologers keep discovering subtle, new ways the moon's influence is felt in our daily lives. The position of the moon in your horoscopes enhances your sun sign. It contributes to new forces, elements, and motivations to the personality of your sun sign.

The bond between your moon sign and sun sign personalities is like a marriage. They are in perfect harmony, sometimes. Like a marriage, they have differences that can foster a stronger connection to build a sustainable partnership, with each personality putting their best foot forward. But, like all marriages, the conflict will arise when contrasting traits collide against each other.

If you ever feel like you are in a perpetual battle with yourself, if you ever think that you have dual personalities inside you constantly at war with each other, you can find peace in astrology. Study your moon and sun signs. Discover the negative and positive aspects of these signs and try to identify these special elements in your own personality. You will realize that a better understanding of the factors that motivate you will enable you to be more compassionate with yourself. You will also finally reconcile what has always seemed to a complicated swirl of contradictions.

Meanwhile, if your moon and sun sign are the same, you will discover that the sign traits are manifested twice as strong in your personality.

Know thyself. That is the inscription carved by the ancient Greeks on the temple walls at Delphi. It is a phenomenon that has baffled humans for more than a thousand years. Astrology is the key.

The Virgo Moon

Having the moon in Virgo influences your sun sign in two ways:

On the plus side, you are meticulous, determined, intelligent, resourceful, and responsible. The downside is, you can be a hypochondriac, judgmental, overly critical, cold, argumentative, and high strung.

The Virgo sign stabilizes the shifting outcome of the moon. Virgo, being the sign of logic and intelligence, gives an acute analytical bend to the moon's impact. If you have your moon in Virgo, your mind is refined and discriminating. You don't seek knowledge for knowledge's sake; there must be a use or relevance of the knowledge you aim to acquire.

Your instinctive response to the sensory information you receive from your environment is to analyze everything you see and hear. You like to take as much as you need to go through the information while questioning everything you obtain. You are such a skeptical personality that you tend to disapprove of things, even if they are right in front of you. You enjoy discussing ideas and digging deep into other opinions, even though external notions do not easily influence you.

You are not a stubborn person per se; you are simply very attached to a theory until proved wrong by facts. You like to seek the truth, being a firm believer that truth is the only remains after the exposure of falsehoods. You're definitely not the person who views life through wine-colored glasses. This doesn't make you pessimistic or sour; you simply address life as it is. This practicality and realism is the reason you are so great with money and business. You see, the big picture rather than the momentary satisfaction, and you worry more about security and providing for your old age.

Having your moon in Virgo is the reason that extra sprinkle of professionalism and perfectionism in every task you engage in. You prefer to take a methodical approach to issues, figuring out the exact solution, and dealing with the problem one step at a time. But your tendency to worry, fuss over every possible negative outcome, and waste time thinking up many contingencies is a little frustrating. You are of the belief that too much productive effort can be destroyed by the absence of the last tiny effort, so you are extremely hard on yourself and others.

You live a life of complete discipline, which can be suffocating. You are the person who would leave their shirt buttoned all the way to the very top, even if it's very uncomfortable but looks perfect! You have a problem understanding scatterbrained or illogical minds, somewhat weird considering how drawn you are to Pisces. Anyway, believe that such people are straight out of a Disney cartoon. You are not only very picky with your choice of friends, but you are also the same way about the cultural activities you participate in.

Your moon sign is responsible for that judgmental quality that follows you almost everywhere. You never miss an opportunity to learn from experience. Women born under this moon sign are sometimes perceived to be unfeminine because they exhibit certain qualities that many don't see as feminine - thoroughness, efficiency, and orderliness.

All Virgo moon people are reserved despite their gender. They also shy away from unnecessary gushiness and sentimentality and are usually considered standoff-ish. The truth is it's the uncivilized Virgo who displays stingy pettiness, picks people apart, and is standoff-ish.

Generally, people with their moon in Virgo show their generosity and care through practical means. You can always rely on them. The sign of service is Virgo, and moon Virgos are just itching to be useful.

Regardless of what your sun sign might be, the lunar Virgo qualities of seriousness and caution manifest in your personality. Your industrious and practical nature is even twice reinforced if your sun sign is one of the Earth signs. You also have a healthy relationship with money.

If you have your sun in a fire sign, the lunar moon manifests endurance and strength to assist your unreserved creativity. This combination is great for politicians and performers. If you have your sun in an air sign, the lunar moon grants you an even more acute intellect and a flair for authenticity. If you have your sun in a water sign, you are bestowed with a more expansive dimension to your emotional personality because you are gifted with a rare mix of hardheaded realism and psychic truth. No matter what your sun sign is, your moon in Virgo grants your acute mental abilities and an intellectual and practical approach to situations.

Celebrities with their Moon in Virgo

1. Amy Adams (American actress)
2. Alice Dellal (Brazilian model)
3. Anna Paquin (Canadian actress)
4. Elizabeth Moss (American Actress)
5. Madonna (Singer and songwriter)
6. Bella Hadid (American model)
7. Blake Lively (American actress)
8. Donatella Versace (Italian fashion designer)
9. Dolly Parton (Singer)
10. Jodie Foster (American actress)
11. Gal Gadot (Israeli actress)
12. J. K. Rowling (British writer)
13. Chelsea Handler (American comedian)
14. Kate Bosworth (American actress)
15. Nicki Minaj (Singer and songwriter)
16. Barbara Stanwyck
17. Serena Williams (American tennis player)
18. Linda Evangelista (Fashion model)
19. Elle Fanning (American actress)
20. Natalie Portman (American actress)
21. The Olsen Twins (Fashion designers)
22. Carey Mulligan (American actress)
23. Michelle Williams (American actress)

24. Jada Pinkett Smith (African-American actress)

25. Joss Stone (Singer and songwriter)

Chapter Ten: Virgo and the Planets

We all know about the solar system. We go to bed at night with the certainty that morning will come again, same time tomorrow. This trustworthy pattern is not only responsible for our day; it also marks our seasons, years, and even our lives. Our adherence to these universal laws allows us to determine the planets' past, present, and future positions at any given time.

Each celestial body in our solar system moves at a different rate and velocity in its own orbit or path. This makes it possible to have an endless supply of unique combinations of planet placements in the sky. The moment you were born, the sun, moon, and all the planets were in specific positions, creating a specific arrangement in the sky. This particular combination will not be seen again for at least four million years. There will not be another human with an identical horoscope as yours seen on Earth for four million years. That person will not be the same as you because of the varying environmental and genetic factors.

How about multiple births, you might wonder? They should have the exact same solar combination, right? Wrong. The ascendant moves by a degree every four minutes. Technically, twins born with as little time as four minutes between them will have their ascendants in two very different zodiacs if one twin broke through during the ending of ascendant and the other at the start of a new one. Even a difference as insignificant as a degree, right in the same Ascendant, will manifest different qualities in the two babies. The minute the Ascendant moves, it produces a different birth chart.

What about people born on the same day and at the same second, maybe even at the same location? These people are called time-twins or astral twins. A lot of time is now being funneled into research on the life-patterns of astral-twins. The results so far are mind-blowing. It has been recorded that time-twins have eerily similar life patterns. There are many cases of them getting married on the same day, having the same mobile number, and even the same genders of children. There are those that are even known to have traveled, relocated, quit jobs, and divorced simultaneously. A few even die simultaneously and with the same cause of death.

Clearly, astral-twins are extremely rare. The distinctive position of the sun, moon, and all the planets in your birth chart is most likely particular to only you. You might have your Sun in Scorpio or Leo, but you differ completely from any other Scorpio or Leo. Imagine how many distinctive fingerprints exist in the world. That's about how many individual horoscopes there are as well. Suppose you intend to obtain more information on the influences of the planets in your life. In that case, you must know the various positions of the planets and their individual influences before applying this knowledge to your personalized birth chart.

Every planet can influence astrology in very specific ways. Each planet rules over a particular aspect of your personality or outlook on life. For instance, Mercury oversees your mental outlook, while Venus is ruler over all things desire.

The manifestations of these different aspects of your personality depend on the placement of these celestial bodies. If the placement of your Mercury is Gemini, you are likely to be quick-witted and talkative. If your Mercury happened to be in Capricorn, your efficiency when handling a project's details or carefully plotting plans beforehand would be legendary.

If your Venus is placed in Leo, you will not be content until you are showered with more attention than you can ever need from a partner. If your Venus falls into Aquarius, you will be of the belief that the freedom to express oneself is one of the most important building blocks of a romantic relationship.

Virgo Ascendant/Rising

At the exact moment you were born, there was a point on the eastern horizon called your Rising sign or Ascendant. The Sun is responsible for your conscious actions and reactions, and the Moon handles the past and your subconscious tendencies.

But the Ascendant is responsible for your instinctive response to your environment, particularly if there are new elements involved. It is concerned with the way you interact with the outside world by merging all the energies in your sun and moon signs, and the rest of your natal chart. Everything that happens is filtered through your Rising sign, indicating the core function of your soul.

People with Virgo Ascendant are usually a little too modest in their appearance and personal mannerisms, although much depends on the placement of their ruling planet, Mercury, on their birth chart. There is a generally reserved but intelligent aura about them that is impossible to miss. These somewhat shy individuals need time to analyze as many elements in their environment as they are comfortable with, before warming up to new people and circumstances. This trait can be perceived as exactly that or as judgmental and standoffish.

This position comes with heightened physical awareness. People born in Virgo rising are acutely aware of their body and its responses to any external and internal stimuli. They pick up on these signals faster than any other Ascendant. Several them are especially fascinated by and interested in physical health. They have a tendency to find comfort and peace in mind-body consciousness exercises like yoga. They are also very passionate about food, although they can be very nitpicky about what to eat and where because they devote a good amount of attention to what they put on and in their bodies.

As is typical with Virgo, these natives have a penchant for worry, especially when facing new territory, situations, and people. They are drawn to people in need of help – or is it the other way around? Therefore, their relationships may have an air of confusion at first, especially due to the Virgo's aversion for messiness... and what is messier than emotions?

Many people with Virgo Ascendants are known for their quiet charm. But, once they've been given the necessary space and time to warm up to their environment, you will realize how much they bring to the table. They make incredibly loyal friends who will go several miles out of their way to help you. It is normal to feel surprised by the modesty hidden beneath a distant and critical first appearance.

The rising sign or Ascendant is usually called the mask we wear when we're exposed to new information and people. More accurately put, it is the instinctive response to our immediate environment. Our Ascendant reveals our natural security and day-to-day coping mechanisms.

As mentioned above, the Virgo Rising natives' traits are also influenced and modified by the location of the planetary ruler of the Ruling sign. For instance, if you were born with a Pisces Ascendant, with Venus, the planetary ruler, in Gemini, you will react to your environment differently from a person with Pisces Ascendant with Venus in Scorpio.

More on Virgo Rising

With your Ascendant in Virgo, you strive to perform every task skillfully with precision, caution, attention to detail, a perfect sense of craftsmanship, and perfectionism. You have a keen sense of observation and have a sharp sensitivity to every single element in your immediate environment. This ensures that you tend to little things that might seem negligible to someone with a different Ascendant. You notice everything, no matter how subtle. You see into the fine grains of life.

Your only desire stronger than your need for perfection is your desire to be of service and assist as many people as you humanly can, most likely in a modest, understated, pedestrian fashion. You are interested in charity for truly helping others rather than for glory or personal recognition. Your basic yearning to be of use and service, your readiness to participate in ongoing practices aimed at improving those lives around you, your readiness to change, or adapt to your circumstances all enable you to always make a positive impact wherever you go.

Also, whenever you feel physically out of balance, you obsess and worry about your health, which only works to worsen your issues. Anyway, all these are simply general characteristics associated with the Virgo Ascendant.

Virgo Ascendant with Mercury in the Signs

Mercury in Aries and Virgo Rising: Mercury is your ruling planet, and it is in Aries. This is an indication of an acute intellect combined with an intuitive handle on situations and the capacity to stand your ground. Your mind is creative and always buzzes with authentic plans and ideas. You can be very impatient, and it shows during conversations with people of duller and slower wits.

You also have a tendency to be aggressive and too argumentative if you are sure that you are right. You are usually found dominating conversations, with little or no receptivity. You are also not very good at listening. Remember that this interpretation is independent of the other factors in your natal chart, which might suggest receptivity to other opinions. You are usually sought as a symbol of authority in your field of expertise.

Mercury in Taurus and Virgo Rising: Your planetary ruler, Mercury, is in the very humble, grounded, and sympathetic sign of Taurus. This indicates that you would rather provide practical service than an emotional one. You ooze efficiency and orderliness, only thinking in very pragmatic, realistic, and logical terms. You have a thing for math or finding a solution to issues with definite, straightforward answers instead of abstract, intangible, and open-ended ones. You are drawn to simplicity, common-sense, and logic as opposed to abstract and complicated.

You are one of the most patient people in the world, with the ability to handle mundane, repetitive, or stressful tasks. If other factors in your natal chart suggest imagination or creativity, you will still have a hard time ignoring the solid or Earthly side of things. If any part of you leans towards art, it is usually the utilitarian, practical, and functional kind of artwork. Concrete data, information, and facts are your specialty.

Mercury in Gemini and Virgo Rising: Your planetary ruler, Mercury, is in the spirited, quick and lively sign of Gemini. This indicates high levels of intellect and mental activity. It is safe to say that you are excited about everything. You absorb new ideas at once and react quickly to changing circumstances and needs. You enjoy organizing information and ideas or simplifying communication for better understanding. This could be an important area of your career or the services you give.

There's a good chance of you becoming a librarian, writer, editor, manager of a fast-paced work environment, or computer scientist. You suffer from nervous stress when you engage in excess mental activity. It would benefit you to pump the breaks a little to calm your nervous system and preserve your health. You also have a fast metabolism. Lucky you!

Mercury in Cancer and Virgo Rising: Your planetary ruler, Mercury, is in the subjective and sympathetic sign of Cancer. This indicates an interest in the healing arts, specifically children's and women's health. You are also passionate about food and nutrition, teaching, and human psychology. You have a tendency to overthink situations, leading to unnecessary worry and anxiety. You are long overdue for a meditation lesson, which will help you release all that pent up tension and anxiety.

You also have a penchant for criticizing the people you care about, especially if you think it is for their benefit. Your specialty lies in the domestic arts, especially because they are also your way of contributing to society.

Mercury in Leo and Virgo Rising: Your planetary ruler, Mercury, found its way into the self-expressive and creative sign of Leo. It indicates frequent use of your creativity, ability to communicate kindly, dramatically, and even colorfully. All these are important aspects of your primary function. You have a tendency to edit and censor the childlike, spirited, and artistic areas of your personality. This will only hide your light, and you were born to shine as brightly as you can.

Mercury in Virgo and Virgo Rising: Your planetary ruler, Mercury, is also in Virgo. This indicates a stable mind with an inclination for apparent logical analysis, classification, and designation. You have a penchant for developing specialized techniques and abilities in a practical field. But, unless other factors in your natal chart indicate an inkling of understanding or vision, you have a tendency to forget everything else in hot pursuit of the tiniest detail. You usually find yourself lost in an abundance of facts and data, which usually renders you incapable of perceiving the overall meaning or direction of things.

Mercury in Libra and Virgo Rising: Your planetary ruler, Mercury, has found itself in the unbiased, judicious sign of Libra. This is a strong indication of diplomacy and the ability to communicate your criticisms, logic, and observations as tactfully as possible.

You are very humble and impartial, with an uncanny ability to see things from an objective viewpoint and give unbiased feedback. This gives you a reputation for a good arbitrator or mediator. You find the logical, practical, and rational nature of science very appealing. You are also an ardent lover of aesthetics, form, and beauty.

Mercury in Scorpio and Virgo Rising: Your planetary ruler, Mercury, is in intellectual Scorpio. This is an indicator you have sharp and powerful perceptions and a strong capacity for research, probing analysis, and detection. You value discretion and are good at keeping secrets. You lean towards barbed-wit, negative criticism, and bitter or dark humor.

Mercury in Sagittarius and Virgo Rising: Your planetary ruler, Mercury, has landed in Sagittarius, the sign of idealism. This means you have solid beliefs, opinions, convictions, and philosophical ideas you keep to your heart. These ideas are the building blocks of your view of life.

You are of the notion you know what is best for everybody, which leads to criticism, usually unsolicited, and frustration. You set the bar impossibly high for yourself, which can lead to bouts of anger and disappointment.

Your sensitive and highly strung nervous system is responsible for the regular holistic habits that calm you and, in turn, others around you.

Mercury in Capricorn and Virgo Rising: Mercury, your planetary ruler, is in Capricorn, the sign of detachment. This makes you a symbol of objectivity, clarity, discrimination, and even-mindedness. Your detached persona gives you an outlook on life is devoid of passion, and while this might sound like a bad thing, it grants you focus like nothing else.

You are not the easiest to flatter or be swayed by flamboyant acts of courtship. Your specialty is discernment and realism. You are drawn to simplicity, order, and structure, as they are the values that guide your entire life.

Mercury in Aquarius and Virgo Rising: Mercury, your planetary ruler, has found its way into the innovative and inventive sign of Aquarius. This indicates your willing to help and serves others, which may be manifested in suggestions of new ideas and concepts.

Your ability to think outside the box is one of your most prized and defining qualities. You are usually fascinated by the unconventional areas like unorthodox health care or methods or healing.

Mercury in Pisces and Virgo Rising: Mercury, your ruling planet, is in Pisces, the sign of receptivity and sensitivity. This indicates your ability to pay attention deeply and truly, be empathetic, compassionate, and serving. You have a poetic imagination and a readiness to be inspired, and this balances your technique and keen attention to detail. Here, you become the technician and the artist.

Conclusion

"My best can surely be better."

Dearest Virgo, these are words by which you live. Your graceful, albeit obsessive, and harmonious nature makes you one of the most admired signs of the Zodiac. You are a firm believer that anything good can be transformed into something great, and these qualities push you even higher than your standards. Your wit and intensity is unmatched, which is why it isn't surprising to find your friends running to you, their walking encyclopedia.

You, Virgo, are famous for your grace and ability to negotiate your way out of the stickiest situations. But your unyielding wish for perfection makes you one of the most challenging personalities yet.

It is completely understandable to demand excellence, but it is also necessary to apply a touch of compassion. Go with the wind sometimes because there's a good chance of ending up somewhere extremely exciting! Always remember that.

Now we've come to the end of this book; I hope you've been able to see yourself for who you truly are. I hope that somehow, you know what to do to work on your messy bits — and there's nothing wrong with messy bits, dear Virgo! We all have them. It's part of the human experience, and the mess isn't going anywhere.

On that note, understand that you are flawed, and that is perfectly fine. Love yourself more. Be more open and accept that you are really amazing as you are. You are special. You are loved. Even with your flaws, you are perfect.

Here's another book by Mari Silva that you might like

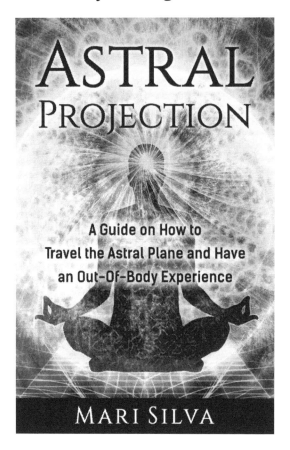

Your Free Gift (only available for a limited time)

Thanks for getting this book! If you want to learn more about various spirituality topics, then join Mari Silva's community and get a free guided meditation MP3 for awakening your third eye. This guided meditation mp3 is designed to open and strengthen ones third eye so you can experience a higher state of consciousness. Simply visit the link below the image to get started.

https://spiritualityspot.com/meditation

References

12 Astrology Zodiac Signs Dates, Meanings and Compatibility. (n.d.).

Astrology - All Sun Moon Combinations. (n.d.). Astrology-Numerology.Com.

Astrology Library. (n.d.). Astrolibrary.Org.

Birth Chart Interpretations -Planets in Signs and Houses. (n.d.). Astrolibrary.Org. https://astrolibrary.org/interpretations/

Cafe Astrology .com. (n.d.). Cafeastrology.Com. http://cafeastrology.com

Horoscope and Astrology - Homepage. (2019). Astro.Com. http://astro.com

The Best Online Astrology Resources. (n.d.). https://bangtanastrology.tumblr.com/post/169791137127/the-best-online-astrology-resources

Printed in Great Britain
by Amazon